Nurse SPARKS: Nurse Stories to Illuminate, Inspire and Ignite

Printed in the United States of America
Editing by Allison Saia

Positive Media Press
4257 Barger Drive, PNB #472
Eugene, OR 97402

www.positivemediapress.com
ISBN: 978-0-692-86660-3
LCCN: 2017940110

NURSE
SPARKS

Nurse Stories to Illuminate, Inspire and Ignite

COMPILED BY
ANITA STEWART, RN
AND AUTHENTIC MESSENGERS

FOREWORD BY
LYNN KEEGAN, PHD, RN, AHN-BC, FAAN

Contents

Foreword

Nurses are the heart, soul, and backbone of the American healthcare system. The numbers alone speak to the relevance of nurses. Currently, there are approximately 3,184,283 Registered Nurses. In contrast, there are less than one-third of that number of physicians, 926,118. In addition, the nursing profession has an additional 827,868 Licensed Practical Nurses, making nurses the largest group of all health and illness professionals. There are three nurses to every one physician, but it is who we are, where we are, how we are and why we are that make nurses so important in the wheel of whole person care.

From entry into planet earth, throughout our earthly journey and at our final transition, the nurse is present, the one who guides and facilitates the miracle of birth and the one who comforts and aids those in their final departure through death from this temporal, physical plane. Throughout the human lifespan the nurse considers all aspects of his or her charge: the body, mind and spirit and often is the most significant health care provider to someone who is suffering, seeking, ill, diseased, or in any kind of mental, spiritual and/or physical need of comfort, guidance or healing.

The question is, are all nurses the same? Do the above characteristics apply to all nurses? Unfortunately, the fact is that they do not. Over several decades the motivation for becoming a nurse has shifted. The desire to alleviate human suffering and care for others use to be the primary reason one pursued a nursing degree rather than say teaching or homemaking, the primary fields open to women mid-20th century. Then with economic shifts and the liberation of women to choose careers in fields other than teaching and nursing, education options burgeoned. Along with those changes recently we have seen an exponential explosion of online degree programs as well as a fluidity of work schedules. Due to these factors, the advent of men in the profession and other societal changes, we have witnessed a change in who goes into nursing and why. The motivation that was once the primarily altruistic desire to help others oftentimes morphed into an economic job security and flexible work schedule job choice. True today many still hold their professions ancestral motivation altruism heritage trait, but many are driven by more practical, external, economic forces. Subsequently and even historically, there are those in nursing whose focus is just getting through the shift and getting their paycheck. Most are not only full-time workers, but also full-time mothers and/or family caregivers, giving out more than they have, running out of steam and sorrily, short on caring. It is not the purpose of this book to address these issues, but rather to witness some of the extraordinary nurses who have overcome many obstacles and have emerged with that generational inner light as well as a practicing vision for a healthier future.

The 16 nurses featured in this edition of *Nurse SPARKS* represent nurses who have achieved inner strength and wisdom through honing their skills and mind-body-spirit focus to deliver excellent, holistic care. Each of these nurses is uniquely different in their education, their area of practice and their approach, but collectively they share the vision of health and healing to each client, patient, and group with whom they interact.

What we know is that it is not how many people we work and interact with that matters. Rather it is the intention and quality of care we render to those individuals, or collection of people, in our day to day presence. The 16 persons featured in this book are the kind of nurses that all of us would be privileged to have as our caregivers. They serve as examples to all of us.

Lynn Keegan, PhD, RN, AHN-BC, FAAN
Director, Holistic Nursing Consultants
Port Angeles, Washington

Lynn Keegan, PhD, RN, AHN-BC, FAAN

Lynn Keegan is one of the founders of the holistic health focus in nursing and a well-known leader in holistic nursing. She currently works as Director of Holistic Nursing Consultants in Port Angeles, WA and has authored or co-authored 21 books and scores of professional journal publications and chapters in textbooks. Her books include seven editions of the co-authored, four-time AJN award-winning book of the year text, *Holistic Nursing: A Handbook for Practice, 7th ed.* (2016); a co-authored book, *The Golden Room: A Practical Guide for Death with Dignity* (2013) North Charleston, SC, and a co-authored two-time AJN award-winning book of the year selection, *End of Life: Nursing Solutions for Death with Dignity* (2011) New York City: Springer Publishers, Inc. Some of her other books include: *Healing Nutrition, 1st and 2nd ed.; Healing with Complementary and Alternative Therapies; Healing Waters: The Miraculous Health Benefits of Earth's Most Essential Resource; Profiles of Nurse Healers,* and *The Nurse as Healer* among others. She served as editor for a 15 book series at Delmar Publishing in the 1990's. In addition, she has delivered scores of presentations and keynote addresses in numerous countries throughout the world.

Dr. Keegan was elected as a Fellow of the American Academy of Nursing and is board certified as Advanced Holistic Nurse by the American Holistic Nurses Association (AHNA). She is past president of AHNA and has been on the board of many organizations and journals. She served on the faculty of several prominent universities including Temple University, Medical University of South Carolina, Texas Women's University and University of Texas Health Science Center, San Antonio, and taught in associate degree programs through coordinating graduate nursing programs. In 1991 she received the Distinguished Alumnus Award from Cornell University – New York Hospital School of Nursing, and later was awarded The Holistic Nurse of the Year by the American Holistic Nurses Association. She is a six-time recipient of the prestigious American Journal of Nursing Book of the Year Award and is primarily known for her contributions to the development and advancement of holistic nursing and in more recent years her work on evolving end of life care.

Find more about her work at www.GoldenRoomAd-vocates.org

Learn about Lynn and her books at https://www.amazon.com/author/lynnkeegan

Preface

The body's energies are the key to vitality, health, and well-being. Energy medicine is the art and science of working with and teaching people to work with these energies to empower them to live happier, healthier lives. Recognized by Eastern cultures, subtle energy fields are only recently being detected, studied, and utilized by Western medicine. It is transforming health care, as well as having an impact on education, business, and sports.

Energy Medicine is among many of the alternative therapies being practiced in hospitals worldwide, (Healing Touch, Therapeutic Touch, Donna Eden energy medicine, Reiki, Pranic healing, etc.) and enables one to offer comfort and relief when nothing else seems to help. There are many books written on the subject, including *Energy Medicine: The Scientific Basis* (Oschman, 2000). The growing number of people turning to alternative therapies is increasing and becoming more and more the chosen form of medical treatment among Americans. One out of every three Americans uses some form of alternative medicine. Between 1990 and 1997 there was a 47 percent increase in visits to alternative practitioners, from 427 million to 629 million, bypassing the estimated total number of visits made to all conventional primary care doctors in 1997. "Today, energy medicine is officially recognized by the U.S. healthcare systems as a sub-specialty within the larger field of Complementary and Alternative Medicine (CAM). The National Center for Complementary and Alternative Medicine (NCCAM), a center within the National Institutes of Health (NIH), is the federal government's lead agency for scientific research on CAM. NCCAM's mission is "to explore complementary and alternative healing practices in the context of rigorous science, and to disseminate authoritative information to professionals and the public." NCCAM's budget had risen from 2 million dollars in 1993, when it was originally called the Office of Alternative Medicine, to $121.6 million in 2008." (Foundation for Alternative and Integrative Medicine)

Nurses practicing Energy Medicine are commending the vote announced recently by NANDA (North American Nursing Diagnosis Association) approving the "Imbalanced Energy Field" nursing diagnosis, submitted in 2016 by the AHNA NANDA-I Energy Task Force. This nursing diagnosis will support registered nurses utilizing energy modalities and allow documentation of clients' responses.

Many of the nurse authors in this book practice some form of Energy Medicine or transpersonal modalities using tools like Tarot or Astrology. Contained in this book are personal stories that will reveal to the reader the many reasons nurses are drawn to complementary practices.

Introduction

NURSES ARE THE HEART OF HEALTHCARE

This book is about nurses and how nursing changed their lives. It's about what it takes to be a nurse, how we came to practice the way we do, and the many lives we have touched.

The idea for *Nurse SPARKS* came to me from what I have come to know as a "Spiritual Download." It happened the night before our launch of the book, *LifeSPARKS* on August 12, 2016. As I lay in bed, head just hitting the pillow, I heard CLEARLY, "And now you will create a book called *Nurse SPARKS*, and it will be an anthology of powerful nursing stories. You need only get the word out to nurses, and those who are listening to their hearts will be drawn to be a part of this book." When these very strong messages come to me, there is only one thing to do...listen and take action. Working with Tami Blodgett on the previous book, *LifeSPARKS* (Amazon best seller), was such a joy and thrill that it just made sense to create *Nurse SPARKS*.

I called Tami the next morning and said, "Hey, what do you think about a book called *Nurse SPARKS*?" "Let's run with it," was her answer. And so it began. It was simple: no attachment to who, or how many nurses would heed the call. I trusted that those who were to be in the book would listen to their inner heart and say 'yes.' The search began in Charlotte, NC, at the Healing Touch Worldwide

Conference. With fliers in hand, I shared the idea with many attendees and saw an amazing amount of interest. It was not long before the book was filled with committed nurses. It came as no surprise that the book was co-authored by nurses with holism as a core belief. Some are pioneers in their fields of expertise, and share their vision, within these pages, about the myriad of ways nurses can have profound effects on the healing of our patients, clients, and the general public.

Working in either a hospital or out-patient surgery center most of my life, I have learned from my profession how to be a "good" nurse. But the "WHY" of what brings us into nursing is what I want to focus on. First and foremost, nursing is one of the most trusted professions on the planet. To quote Lynn Keegan in the foreword, "The desire to alleviate human suffering and care for others use to be the primary reason one pursued a nursing degree." But times have changed. The characteristic of altruism may be fading, but what I see from hindsight and a long career at the bedside is; compassion is the core value that is re-shaping our profession. As Thomas Merton wrote: "Compassion is the keen awareness of the interdependence of all things." As nurses become more compassionate, their ability to provide better care grows substantially." As you will see in the following stories, these nurse authors bare their hearts with you the reader.

Looking back, I feel tremendous gratitude for my eclectic career. I have felt good, bad, high, low and every emotion on the scale from 0-10. I have left work in tears, prayed for a miracle or two, hated my job, and loved it. At times, feeling like my gut was clenched in a vise and I could not go to work one more day, I searched for ways to deal differently with my job. Most of the time, when distressed, I found my focus was ego-centered versus heart-centered. When I could put myself in the place of the patients, seeing through their eyes, treating them like they were a family member, then I felt deeply rewarded. When I was complaining about how bad the hospital was, how over-tasked and underpaid we were for what we do, how under-staffing was creating dangerous sentinel events and putting my license on the line, I felt horrible...in fact, I would threaten to quit. "It's just not worth it anymore," would be the rhetoric. I had to find a balance: one that would honor my needs and those of the patients. Journeying into a deep Spiritual path was my answer. "Seek ye first the Kingdom within, and all else will be added unto you." I found this path to be my saving Grace. Only when we can have compassion, will we step out of egoic needs and base our actions, thoughts, words and deeds on Love. Compassion is the essence of nursing.

With a heart full of Love, I invite you to sit back and enjoy reading the following stories.

Anita Stewart, RN
Owner, Bridges of the Heart

"The ability to recognize yourself in the archetypes is at the foundation for competence with tools that make use of the archetypes. Only when you begin to identify archetypal patterns and their expressions in your own life can you hope to use the tools that work with archetypes in a therapeutic session."

—Toni Gilbert, *Gaining Archetypal Vision*

CONSCIOUS ARCHETYPAL ENERGY AND HEALING

TONI GILBERT, RN(RET), MA, ATC

My first introduction to archetypal energy was a mystical one. It was a profound encounter that occurred in my twenties, and because of that experience ---and a gauntlet of life's teachings in the years that followed---I see the world, and myself in a more comprehensive and holistic way.

At twenty-eight, my spirituality was maturing. I could see that everything was too beautiful, too complex and too well designed to be accidental. I sincerely wanted to know more about the creator of the world in which I lived.

Staying open to all possibilities, I prayed, "Who are you that have made this place?"

I didn't get an answer right away, so I asked and asked and asked for I was determined to receive an answer. I waited. I read. I sewed, and I cooked. I took care of my children, meditated, practiced yoga, ate healthy food, and listened to music. All the while, I searched with my senses. Still, there was no response.

After about a month of continually asking, "Who are you?" an answer finally came. Suddenly I felt a loving and compassionate presence, much like a softly flowing river. I immediately knew this was the spiritual answer that I had been asking for because it was more intensely loving than anything I had felt in ordinary life. The Spirit's flowing unconditional love and deep compassion gently surrounded my body. At the same time, it ran through my heart center at the middle of my chest while it caressed my cheek like a gentle summer's breeze.

The experience was multi-sensory. Without words, the Spirit telepathically communed. It was aware of me, loved me and had compassion for my struggles. I heard a sound much like a choir of angelic sopranos holding a steady note --a feminine "Auuuumm." At the time, I knew nothing of the Aum sound or its origins. I later learned of its use in Buddhism and other oriental meditative practices. Buddhism like many patriarchal religions is based upon men's experiences. The Aum, often heard in the meditative traditions, is of a masculine tone but mine was feminine.

For about a minute, this Spirit communicated not in words, but with a felt knowing that "It" was what I called "God." It needed neither name nor gender and had neither beginning nor end. My intelligence seemed small compared to the intelligence of this Spirit, and I knew I did not have the capacity to know It completely.

Because of this mystical communion, I have come to know our Creator as an intelligent and conscious energy, the archetypal pattern of a loving Spirit.

Since that time, I have spent many hours exploring how to tap into this archetypal energy at various levels of consciousness. The exploration of dreams, imagery and meditation are internal techniques that bridge unconscious information with the ego, whereas the art of Tarot cards and other forms of art expression are external techniques. The symbolic and synchronistic magic I have observed while using these healing tools has changed my culturally conditioned ideas of materialistic separateness from God/Spirit to a more inclusive vision. I see and feel an energetically connected world.

The body contains conscious energy, and this energy flows through the body much like a river, complete with multiple chakras or points of energy concentration. We move this energy with our thinking and our intention. It is replete with archetypal patterns of information that we can access depending upon our level of consciousness, affect, body postures, facial expression and---even the clothes we wear. I see this spiritual world through my inner vision and feel it with my energy body. To me, this spiritual world is a reality that has become an intrinsic part of my transpersonal counseling practice. I believe that every person has a similar spiritual core and that each of us can tap into that Spirit to enhance our work and lives.

Throughout history, many people have explored this energy of consciousness and attempted to map and diagram it for others. Sigmund Freud, for example, identified various levels of the human consciousness. Both he and Carl Jung thought that the mind's consciousness contained levels of information about who we are personally and collectively and that we could access this information through logical thinking and intuitive insights.

When working with the art on Tarot cards, the images we see tap into archetypal levels of consciousness within us. The questioner first views the image on the card allowing his or her memories to rise to consciousness. I encourage them to free associate. When the person has no more to say, I offer an intuitive interpretation of the card. This interpretation also taps into a place in their consciousness where they know the truth of a situation. When this happens, insights burst forth in a wellspring of answers for the questioner.

Twenty-eight-year-old Melissa sought wellness counseling due to two physical ailments: chronic constipation and vaginal irritation. She was scheduled to see a traditional physician and decided to make an appointment with me to explore her body's wisdom. Her life was in constant flux. Melissa worked odd jobs, traveling around the state and abroad. She had a partner, but it was a sexual paring, each going their separate ways after a once-a-week get-together.

Because of the location of her symptoms we discussed her body issues as they related to the first two chakras. The first chakra has to do with sex and other survival of the species issues. The second chakra deals with reproduction, but also contains stored information about the culture and the family of origin. At the physical level, I taught her about how depression can slow the bowels causing constipation.

We then turned to the Tarot cards. Melissa chose the Voyager Tarot deck. The faces of the cards in this deck have photographic collages depicting modern life. Clients easily identify with the symbolism. She asked the question: "What do I need to know to help me with my health issues?"

The first card, of a four-card spread, was entitled "Regenerator and Sage of Cups." Melissa said 'I see a couple of men tending the earth by pouring water on it. This seems to be addressing my need for nurturance. The two older people in the corner of the card seem like wise counselors." I also saw this card as a reflection of her seeking wise counsel and nurturing, thus supporting her intuitive process.

The second card, entitled "Empress" evoked a strong emotional reaction. "She is spiritually evolved and in tune with all of nature," Melissa said with awe. The card's image was of a golden woman standing proudly in a field of flowers, a snow-topped volcano appeared in the background, and a beautiful waterfall was at her side. An image of the earth with its swirling weather patterns was behind her, and a multi-petaled flower fanned out around her head like a large dramatic crown. To finish the spiritual scene, a white dove of peace flew above it all.

I knew Melissa's consciousness was tapping into and feeling the archetypal energy of the Empress. I asked Melissa to describe where in her body she was feeling the feminine energy. She thought for a moment then, with a sweeping gesture of her hand, she indicated her heart and lower abdomen saying "I feel the Empress' energy at my heart chakra and then all the way down my body."

Melissa's reaction to the Empress archetype included the area of her body that was symptomatic. I thought Melissa would benefit by exploring this image at a deeper level of consciousness. The spontaneous imagery or visualization found at the preconscious level of the self can uncover insights and wisdom beyond the knowing of the conscious ego. I discussed this with her, and she agreed to use a visualization technique to explore the Empress archetype. I had her close her eyes and then led her through a brief relaxation phase. Next, I asked her to allow an image of the Empress to form in her imagination. After a brief pause, Melissa reported she saw the Empress in a quiet forest meadow.

With her eyes still closed, Melissa described the Empress as dressed in a flowing white gown and different from the image on the card. She then internally dialogued with the Empress. The image said, "I am here to assist you in your healing."

Next, I told Melissa to, in her imagination, become the Empress. After a brief quiet meditation in which Melissa embodied the archetype, I asked her to describe her experience. Her affect and voice softened as she talked about ways to live in harmony and "making every step sacred in honor of the earth and all its inhabitants."

As the imagery session came to a close, the Empress told Melissa that she would be available to her anytime she needed advice or support. Melissa needs only to close her eyes with the intention of contacting her and she would be there. When she felt done, I asked her to return to waking consciousness where upon we continued the discussion about how to walk life's path with the integrity and grace of the Empress.

The third card, entitled "Lovers" is the archetype of relationships. She looked at this card for what seemed like a long time. "There are two people in an embrace on the card." Her voice began to trail away as she mentioned some other aspects in a rather superficial way. I then asked her if she wanted to visualize this card too. She issued a sharp "No!" With this response, I decided whatever messages she was getting from this card was very personal, and she wasn't ready to discuss them with me. I respected this and gave her space by talking about the card's interpretation. I told her, "The symbol of the lovers represents different kinds of love, and the choices love calls upon us to make. The Empress makes choices based upon integrity and is true to herself and honest in her relationships."

Intuitively, I put forth a hunch; I said, "Maybe the Empress is calling upon you to make every step a sacred step in your relationships too." Melissa closed her eyes, let out a long sigh and said, "That is just what I needed to hear." We didn't discuss Melissa's love life. Instead, we focused on the wisdom she needed to begin making better choices for herself. I took this receptive time to suggest, "Maybe you wouldn't have vaginal problems if you align your heart and your actions in your relationships." She softly looked me in the eye and nodded yes.

The fourth card was entitled "Guardian and Woman of Crystals." The card shows a woman surrounded by multi-faceted crystals, with one on her forehead. This is the archetype of intuitive and intellectual mastery. This card prompted a discussion around getting out of the head or intellect and listening to the body's wisdom. In my assessment, she was so bombarded with parental, cultural, and commercial values that her ability to "look within for answers" was limited.

Lastly, I began to teach Melissa how to notice valuable innate intuitive impulses and translate them through the equally valuable intellect.

As you can see, when the questioner looks at the cards it is like looking into a mirror. In the card-mirror, symbols cause thoughts and feelings to bubble up from the preconscious and unconscious mind. With the guidance of a trained Tarot counselor, the archetypal energy of the symbols leads the questioner to deep insights necessary for self-development and self-acceptance.

In my experience of Tarot, something happens beyond our everyday awareness to affect the performance of the cards. As in the example of Melissa, the thinking and feeling states of the client synchronistically affect the order of the cards as they are shuffled and placed into a predetermined formation. The layout of the images reflected the psychological profile of Melissa's question.

Synchronicities, which can be viewed as part of our conscious energy structure, manifest in the form of seemingly coincidental occurrences, which symbolically connect our psyches to the events that are happening in the world. Because this does not make logical sense, synchronicity is often experienced as a miracle, serendipity or pure chance.

Synchronistic events disrupt our everyday notions of reality, thus giving us a larger sense of the world in which we live. Indeed, such experiences---which the mystics write about---suggest that there is a direct interaction between the material world and our feelings, behaviors and thoughts. Working with the healing arts such as Tarot, dreams and guided imagery often brings us closer to this mystical realm of experience, one that always enriches the healing potential within.

Since my experience with the spiritual energy, I have read extensively. I have found that the world's religions contain references to it in their traditions and now scientists are validating this ancient energy in the laboratory.

When researchers examine the effects of this energy, they report consistent and remarkable results, and some scientists postulate that we do seem to be a part of something greater than ourselves and in participation with a consciousness beyond ourselves. The words flow and river are often associated with this formless and genderless quantum field of energy.

Essentially, the entire world is energetic and conscious manifested by an intelligent life force or flow of energy that makes up the human form, animals, plants and inanimate objects such as rocks. A similar idea is known in virtually every traditional culture throughout the world. Whether it be Native American, Greek, African, Japanese or Chinese, a life energy is recognized as an entity unto itself. This energetic life force is often described as being like a river with no beginning and no end and is known by various names: Chi, Pneuma, Prana, Qi, Flow, or Spirit.

Whatever the name or the description, it is still the same life force, a flowing creative energy of the universe. We are It. It surrounds and permeates and is every sense, organ, and cell. Like Melissa, we need to realize and honor that we are spiritual energy because to ignore this uniqueness affects our physical, psychological and spiritual health.

Toni Gilbert, RN (ret), MA, ATC

Toni Gilbert, RN (ret), MA, ATC is a transpersonal counselor with a background in holistic nursing. As a professional with a formal education in nursing, psychology, and transpersonal studies, she offers clients an array of healing arts techniques to enhance wellness and prevent illness. She was the editor of the online magazine, *Alternative Journal of Nursing* and the founding director of the Oregon Holistic Nurses Association. Toni is the author of *Messages from the Archetypes: Using Tarot for Healing and Spiritual Growth*, published by White Cloud Press, *Gaining Archetypal Vision: A Guidebook for Using Archetypes in Personal Growth and Healing* by Schiffer Books and *Images of Our Time: A history and pictures of a pioneer family.* She has written for national and local publications and was a guest on multiple radio interviews. You may see her published articles and listen to her radio interviews on her personal website.

www.tonigilbert.com

toni@tonigilbert.com

"Start by doing what is necessary,
then what is possible and suddenly you are
doing the impossible."

—By St. Francis of Assisi

Firm but Compassionate

RUTH KENT RN., CBCP.

"Don't you ever, ever do this to me again" these words penetrated through every cell of my being. It was December 25th, 1998 and the unit (Surgical Intensive Care) where I was working was crazy busy. I happened to see one of the doctors come into the unit; he was rushing around and very loudly calling out some information about one of the patients. Unfortunately, it happened to be information that was not to be shared, especially with some of the family members, who were at the bedside of this patient. I gently went up to this doctor, attempting to give him a clue to be silent. With my finger over my lips, I asked him to please "SHHHHHHH" and to come with me. My intention was to have him step into a room, and I would be able to explain to the doctor the concerns for the privacy and respect of the patient. We stepped into a room, but it did not go smooth or in the direction intended. He came within an inch of my face and looking like he was going to explode. That is when I heard those words, "Don't you ever, ever do this to me again," being blasted out at me.

Initially, I was scared and started to ask God for help. Knowing there had to be something that was behind this outburst I just stood there. I was praying for help. I respected this doctor and chose not to attack or react at this time. Immediately I saw the doctor's look on his face shift. At this point, I believe, he realized what had just taken place and left the unit. There I stood asking myself, "What in the world just happened?" I looked at the patient that was in this room and all the confused, intense feelings I was feeling seem to wither away for the moment. The patient was a young 20-year-old man who just had oral surgery and had his mouth wired shut. His eyes were huge. He couldn't speak, but his face and eyes were speaking volumes. I went up to him and shared that this doctor was under a great deal of tension and everything was OK. I found out later this doctor elected to work 72 hours of trauma call over Christmas. He was Jewish; he was trying to help others out, and work Christmas weekend. I have a saying that seems to fit here "Two wrongs don't make a right." So what do I do now? Say nothing and let it go or report this so that no one is allowed to work 72 hours of trauma call at any time again. I took some time to go within and ask myself what is the best for all in this situation. I did not talk to others about this because I didn't want to get all confused with a lot of opinions.

A few days later, I went directly to the head of the Medical Staff and explained the concerns and the events as they took place. He took in the information and stated he would get back to me in a couple of days. There was protocol he had to take and before proceeding he reconnected with me. I recall sitting in this little room with the Head of the Medical Staff, my Administrative Nurse and myself. It felt like I was in back in school in the Principal's office. He gave me two choices. One he would suspend the doctor for several months, or he would allow the doctor to continue to work, pending a review in two months. I felt that this doctor knew immediately while standing in front of me that day that he was sorry. By me staying firm and yet compassionate, he was willing to make things right. I found out, from a fellow nurse, that when he left the unit so abruptly that day he went out and called his wife. In calling his wife, he told her, "I can't believe what I just did. I yelled at the kindest and most compassionate nurse in the unit." Before long things were back to routine for the doctor and myself and lessons had been learned. By the way, the patient's family never knew anything occurred.

So, what did I take away from this event? Looking back at the 31 years of healthcare and 25 years of Intensive Care nursing, I started to recall a thread that I felt was ingrained within me and helped me to be the nurse I was - RESPECT and INTEGRITY. Every day this thread was the core of my actions; it was a measuring tool for me. Did I do what I could to help this patient, the family of the patient, the staff that I was working with every day? My father and my mother taught me these values as a child. Looking back at the very beginning of my journey in healthcare, I actually fought becoming a nurse. My sister and sister-in-law were both nurses, and my brother-in-law was a nurse anesthetist. I saw their long hours, the hard work and heard the stories they would share. In addition, they had to work holidays and extra hours and be on call at times. Why would I want to do this? During the time I was looking for a path to take after high school, something happened that would set the stage for my career in nursing.

My first J-O-B was as a dishwasher, but I left after only a short time. The only job opening that I could find was a CNA, Certified Nursing Assistant, position in the Nursing Home where my sister-in-law worked. I figured I would do this only until I went to school for something else or a better job showed up. I loved that work, and it was the hardest work I've ever done. I fell in love with nursing. I felt that policy and procedures were guidelines, but it was more important that you carry out your work in love, respect and take that extra step, give that extra moment, and do it all with love. In 1971 I proudly entered an LVN Nursing program. After graduating, I started to work on an Orthopedic floor. In a very short time, I was the charge nurse with a CNA on the night shift of a 20-bed orthopedic surgical unit. I had flashbacks of my dishwashing days and felt, if this is nursing let me out of here! I knew I had to make a change but was uncertain as to where or what that was. At this time, I happened to be visiting my cousin and a neighbor of her's, who worked as an RN. She asked me to come work with her. I didn't have anything to lose, so I went on faith. March of 1973 began my Intensive Care nursing career.

For several years initially working in the SICU, I had to work the night shift. One morning as I was finishing my patient's care, a coworker of mine stuck his head around the curtain to ask me to come to his office when I finished. The co-worker was the Doctor of Pharmacology who oversaw the activities of the unit related to drug and patient relationship. After giving my report to the oncoming nurse and turning over the care of my current patient, I was free to go find out what the Pharmacologist wanted. There he stood in the middle of the unit, as he didn't have an office.

He stated that he had been following me and reviewing my charting for the last three months. I asked if he would mind sharing with me why he was doing this. His response surprised me. "I could not figure out what it was that you were doing to have better cardiac output, less sedation or pain medication, better urinary output, improved vital signs, and better quality rest for your patients. But I now know what it is, it is your bath." I laughed and knew there had to be more. The bath was pretty good; I would put their hands and feet in warm water and do some massaging in these areas. But more importantly, if possible, I would get to know the patient and talk over things of interest with them. Inviting them for a moment to forget they are in a hospital and dealing with the number of challenges that alone can bring. I was hoping to reconnect to a passion or purpose that was within them. When the individual had a drive to get better, something to live for, this was the best medicine in the world. This would create Miracles to happen for them.

Coming from a place of love, showing respect, and meeting the individual where they are at without judgment or criticism, working together with them lovingly, informing them of the steps and why it is important. To be firm on what is a must-do and compassionately educate, support, and listen to them in helping to work together for their benefit. There was one patient that often comes to mind and summed up my nursing approach to each individual the best. This man had never been in a hospital and was not use to not being in control. He was a business owner and clearly the top hierarchy of his business and family. I came into the room, and it was evident that he was angry, frustrated and under all this, scared. Taking a moment to introduce myself, set up a plan and to inquire if this was understood and approved by him. I would do this in small increments and reassess throughout the 12-hour shift. There were some things he did not agree to. After informing him as to the reasoning for this to be done, the support he would be given, and the goal intended to achieve by doing so, he willingly joined me in the efforts. The patient started to see improvement and would request me to be his nurse when I was on duty. At the time of transfer out of the Intensive Care, he asked to be given something to inform my administration of the care he received from me. So, I handed him the index sized card that we had for these messages. He very abruptly stated, "That is not going to be big enough." I came back to work a couple of days later, and there was the note. It was on a letter-sized sheet of paper commenting on the extra care and the respect he felt he had received from me. Then he wrote, "If I would describe Ruth I would say she is Firm but Compassionate."

I retired from nursing in the hospital setting September 21st, 2013, which happened to be the International Day of Peace. I feel I have not actually retired from nursing for I now have an international business from my home assisting individuals with tools and information, specific to their needs to reach their goals of balanced health and happiness. After 41 years of Intensive Care nursing and my own wellness journey, I realized I didn't want to be a category or a diagnosis and felt I didn't treat my patients this way either. First and most importantly, they are a person with emotions and needs. I started to look into ways to heal physically and emotionally, by boosting my innate healing potential that was specific to my needs. I discovered tools that addressed the core of the imbalance physically and emotionally. I am very grateful for learning about energy medicine: the

Nikken Wellness Home technology, the Emotion Code and Body Code, the use of oils and many other tools. It is not only for me that I am grateful. This journey has finally given me an answer to the question I found myself asking many times at the bedside of a patient. "Lord, what else is there that needs to be done for this patient?" Now with the freedom, I Firmly and Compassionately serve, support and inform others of simple, effective, self-help tools. My intention is to carry out research with the Emotion Code to then bring this into mainstream medicine. Bridging the fields of healthcare and to come together to achieve the goals of balanced health and happiness for each individual.

Remember the question I posed to myself when looking into a career: "Why would I do this?" Well, I can tell you why I did and continue to do so. Because I love helping people. I love meeting them where they are and working together to help their today and tomorrow be better in every way possible. Find within you the strength to be Firm but Compassionate. To be firm but compassionate is not only about how you're responding to the environment or to the individuals around you, but it's creating that space within you in the moment, finding that self-respect, the respect of others, the integrity, the authenticity, and the truth coming from a place of love. Choose to create healthy boundaries, come from a place of love, and be firm but compassionate in every moment of your life.

Ruth Kent RN., CBCP.

Ruth Kent RN., CBCP. Emotion Code Seminar Instructor and provides Success Together Program. Ruth worked in healthcare for 47 years, of which included 41 years of Intensive Care Nursing. She loved nursing, and after retiring in 2013, she expanded the opportunity to help others more. The awareness and the means to helping others came to her during a period of challenges in her own life. During this time of physical, emotional, and financial struggles she was introduced to Nikken, Inc. and through Nikken came to know Dr. Brady Nelson. She soon became a client and student of Dr. Nelson's. This brought her to learn and benefit from The Emotion Code and Body Code. Regaining her health and financial status, she also noted to have been gifted with a deeper purpose that filled her with gratitude to have gone through this hard time. Her umbrella for service, specific to each individual, is to provide simple and effective self-help tools that support them where they are and provide tools for a lifetime of benefits. Her intention is to allow each person to discover the means to live a life of joy through freedom.

www.ruthkentllc.com

ruthkentpresent@gmail.com

"Considering the problems facing our world, we vitally need not only new ideas and solutions, but also new ways of thinking about reality itself."

—Marina Ormes

Dancing with the Universe: How Astrology Brings Meaning to the Healing Process

MARINA ORMES RN, HN-BC (RET)

As the daughter of a National Aeronautics and Space Administration (NASA) astrophysicist, I grew up in a household committed to science and rational ways of understanding the world. Everything was logical and made sense. Although my parents were loving people, they had no explanation for things like love, spirituality, why things happened the way they did, or mysteries like life and death.

When I was three years old, my parents left me alone with a babysitter. I was frightened and didn't want my parents to leave. The babysitter comforted me by telling me that God was watching over me. My family was not religious, and while I had heard about God, I had no context for understanding what it meant. So the closest thing my three-year-old self could imagine was that God was something like Santa Claus—a mythical figure who had magical powers to watch over everyone at the same time. Even at age three, I didn't think either Santa Claus or God were real in the sense of someone I could see and talk to, but there was this grown up 17-year old person who really believed this, so I had to make sense of it somehow.

Later, when I was about six, I asked my parents what God was. Their best answer was that God was something some people believed in and others didn't. Well, from people who had a rational explanation for everything, that answer seriously fell short. I wanted to know more.

As an adolescent, I immersed myself in a quest to understand what gives life a greater sense of meaning and purpose. Science had no explanation for incredible mysteries like birth and death. I sought to understand how things like creativity and passion for life and the palpable existence of a bigger picture could coexist with what was presented as a rational, objective world. I ingested stories of escaped slaves and Holocaust survivors in an attempt to understand why people might go on in the face of incredible hardship, and what it was that gave meaning to their lives.

In college, I started out as a biology major interested in a pre-med track, but once again found that a strictly scientific approach to healing left something missing. Illness and injury affected different people in different ways and had a different meaning for each person, and that sense of meaning or purpose could be felt at any stage of physical breakdown or repair. Clearly, healing was about something more than simply fixing the mechanics of the physical body. I wanted to understand better how that worked. But science gave me no language to explain what I noticed—that people had the experience of meaning for things that had no rational explanation.

After college, I was still looking for my path. In the mid-1990's I pursued a comprehensive training program in herbal medicine. As I studied and began practicing this holistic healing modality, I was happy to have tools that could help people in some situations, but I still felt as though something important was missing. What we had done, it seems, was to replace one system (allopathic medicine) that addressed physical needs with another, perhaps gentler, system (herbal medicine) that still was primarily used to instigate physical repair.

What I noticed was that my clients could often be resistant to taking responsibility for their own health care due to deeper emotional patterns not being addressed. For example, preparing and drinking an herbal tea four times a day requires lifestyle changes that many clients were unable to adopt or maintain. Taking herbal remedies may not be effective if someone is unable to quit smoking or has other unhealthy habits. The illness or issue was actually pushing them to face something about themselves they didn't want to look at and were not receiving support for. And I felt intuitively that if needs could be addressed at those deeper levels, the healing could happen more easily regardless of the modality being used.

I feel very fortunate that my teachers in herbal medicine also introduced me to the mysterious worlds of astrology and shamanism—ways of understanding that offered deeper insights and a bigger picture. These frameworks had no legitimate role in a materialistic, scientific worldview and could not be proven by objective standards. But I noticed that they immediately helped my clients find meaning that empowered them to make lasting lifestyle changes. These lifestyle changes went hand in hand with empowering beliefs and attitudes that resulted in greater health and vitality and a positive outlook in life. Also, because each client's experience of life's challenges is spelled out in the symbolic language of the astrological birth chart, clients—through learning about their charts—could accept themselves in ways that allowed them to embrace health and well-being more fully.

By integrating this bigger-picture approach with real-world challenges and problems, I noticed that my clients were able to shift their thinking in ways that opened up new opportunities for both physical healing and personal growth. Difficulties that had previously felt insurmountable began to feel less daunting. An understanding of how problems fit in the context of the meaning and purpose of one's life brought a deeper feeling of peace and fulfillment, along with renewed energy and creative solutions that led to positive changes, regardless of whether their physical problem was "fixed" or not.

In the decades that followed—in both my personal life and in my professional role as a holistic healer, astrologer, birth doula, wedding officiant, and holistic nurse—I deepened my understanding of different layers of meaning (mental, physical, emotional, and spiritual) that can help us understand our experience. I saw the power of describing this meaning through the symbolic world of interpenetrating dynamic cycles that is astrology. And over time this became the focus of my practice and my work with clients.

So what is astrology? Astrology is a framework of understanding and a language that happens to be connected to the cycles of the Sun, Moon, and planets in our solar system. Western astrology—in its evolutionary[1] and archetypal[2] forms—provides a logical, complex pattern of interpenetrating cycles of change that occur within a context of meaning and purpose. Astrology offers a sense of belonging and connection for each and every human being as well as a road map for personal growth and evolution. It conveys a bigger-picture reason for life events and experiences that support positive thinking about the situations in which we find ourselves.

When we learn about the qualities and cycles of planetary movement, we can become more aware of the existence of ongoing natural cycles of evolution and change. We can take advantage of inherent opportunities to transform— opportunities that already exist, both on subjective and objective levels of reality.

In my work with clients over the years, I have found the movement and evolving relationships of the planets through the zodiac to have surprising significance to their experience of life. What strikes me, over and over again, is how profoundly the information in a chart resonates for a client as I speak with him or her. I frequently hear comments like "you are precisely describing what it is like to be me," and "you are describing how I have always felt but never been able to put into words." It isn't that I can predict or "guess" at the exact life experiences a person has had, but more like I can describe the context of those experiences:

---

[1]   Evolutionary astrology is a view of astrology that looks at the "bigger picture" within the natal chart and includes the perspective of the soul—a sense of self that exists prior to and beyond this lifetime.

[2]   Archetypal astrology is astrological symbolism that describes universally experienced patterns that are an integral part of the human psyche. These patterns can be investigated by and can inform the human mind, but can never be fully understood by it.

how they felt, what was important about them, and what they mean for the person and the significance of their life.

For example, I might see in a chart that someone has a highly developed capacity for self-criticism and playing small, or a natural tendency to lead without feeling sure of themselves on the inside, or a need to be proactive in his or her pursuit of a spiritual path that has personal meaning regardless of what he or she has been told. When I share what I am noticing with the client, it creates a space where they can feel validated in their own internal experience, connect with a sense of meaning and context for what they feel, and feel empowered to move forward in their healing and growth with new awareness.

Finding meaning through astrology is not a new concept. Our ancestors were intimately connected to these bodies for reasons that deserve our attention. For ancient people, the movement of the celestial bodies represented predictable systems of calculating and understanding the passage of time. From the daily rising and setting of the Sun to the 29-year cycle of Saturn, eclipse cycles, and relationships of the planets to one another from conjunction to opposition and back to conjunction, the interpenetrating metronomes of the heavenly bodies provided guideposts for understanding the difference between the present, past, and future and placed life's experiences in a bigger picture of meaning and purpose.

Our ancestors did not separate astronomy from astrology. Today, the purpose of astronomy is to understand the cosmos rationally and objectively. Separated from that is the capacity to understand the cosmos as it relates to and interacts with the self. Astrological understanding, on the other hand, uses our knowledge of astronomy to integrate subjective experiences of meaning and connection; therefore, astrology—unlike astronomy—is both rational and irrational, objective and subjective. When used for empowerment, it affects and informs us subconsciously and emotionally as well as consciously and intellectually.

Astrology is a multidimensional system of symbolic understanding that includes the perspective of the individual self (shown by the natal chart), the perspective of the changing cosmos (shown by ongoing planetary cycles), and the perspective of the interaction between the two (shown by transits, or planetary positions and cycles as they relate to the natal chart). By considering the significance with which astrology can impact our lives, we can begin to understand its potential. Ultimately, where astrology takes us is not out into the cosmos but deep within ourselves— to a profound understanding of the power we have to live out the ideals of wisdom and compassion and to create meaningful, fulfilling lives. I believe that astrology can open our minds to hints of the true nature of consciousness and its relationship to the universe.

And in fact, by understanding the evolutionary context in which an illness or condition reveals itself, any provider or practitioner can adopt a more effective holistic and multidisciplinary approach to treatment as well as a more compassionate and supportive response to a patient or client. This approach may or may not bring more rapid alleviation of physical complaints; however—and perhaps of even greater significance—by supporting the client in his or her evolutionary needs, there is a potential to assist or allow a deeper sense of meaning, belonging, and fulfillment of his or her unique life purpose to unfold.

In my role as Director of the Oregon Holistic Nurses Association (OHNA), I have observed a growing awareness of the potential for astrology to inform both practitioner and patient about the nature of the individual's deeper needs and inner experiences. In the future, we may see more holistic practitioners incorporating their knowledge of astrology into their practices to broaden their professional repertoire. A patient can also investigate these cycles to gain a better understanding of his or her health needs. Of course, anyone with health concerns should always seek medical assistance from a licensed practitioner. Astrologers do not make diagnoses or offer medical advice (unless they have additional credentials), but they can and do provide perspective about the bigger picture of personal growth and how health and other challenges play a role in these processes.

Health and physical well-being, as well as health care, can fit into a broader picture of life that incorporates insight originating from an awareness of planetary cycles. These cycles provide a framework for understanding how a life challenge can be seen in the context of personal growth and evolutionary healing in alignment with life purpose. Of course, we could substitute any life challenges—anything that brings about negative states such as anxiety, worry, fear, or depression—and place them in this model and it works just as effectively. Human beings regularly deal with a range of emotional, mental, physical, and spiritual challenges.

In addition to physical health, we all have a wellness spectrum (from barely functional to highly fulfilled) in a variety of life areas such as work, relationships, creative expression, family, identity, spirituality, etc. One individual might be highly functional in relationships but experience large blocks regarding creativity. Another person might come from a dysfunctional family and be very successful in his or her career. Ultimately, as human beings, we are on a path to fulfillment through healing each of these areas of life. We can gain insight into all of these life areas through analysis of the astrology chart and transits. Astrology can provide you with a road map that helps you understand and accept who you are with kindness and compassion. It describes who you are in the depth of your complexity and truth, and empowers you to become all you are capable of becoming.

As far as my life goes, I feel I have come full circle. In the ancient art and science of astrology, I discovered a logical, rational way of understanding human experiences and motivations that incorporates a much wider view of who we are as human beings. It allows us to see our healing and wholeness in an evolutionary context, as a path of purpose that gives meaning to our lives.

Marina Ormes RN, HN-BC (ret)

Marina Ormes is the author of Cycles of Healing: Personal Transformation in Relationship to a Living Cosmos. She is an evolutionary astrologer and a retired board-certified holistic nurse with a background of over 20 years in astrology and holistic healing. She is the Director of the Oregon Holistic Nurses Association and the founder of Astrology Heals.

Marina is certified in evolutionary astrology through the Steven Forrest Apprenticeship Program, and she has a professional background as a labor and delivery nurse, wedding officiant, birth doula, wellness consultant, and professional astrologer. Her interest in healing and what makes human beings feel meaning, joy, and purpose has guided all of her professional pursuits.

Marina serves healing professionals and visionary changemakers by helping them understand themselves better and live the life they are here to live. She supports them in discovering the meaning and purpose that is an essential part of whole-self wellness and helping them make a positive contribution to their communities and the world.

She offers private consultations, small group programs, monthly New and Full Moon guided meditations, classes, and more. She can meet with clients online from anywhere in the world.

cyclesofhealing.com and astrologyheals.com

info@astrologyheals.com

"Life has taught me that being open and willing, curious and courageous, grateful and giving will set the spirit free. Tap into your vibrational energy, realize your potential and live your life with passion. "

—Monica Andrusko

From Burnout to Gratitude

MONICA ANDRUSKO RN, BSN, CNHP

It had been 20 years since I had been to school, yet there I was, in the middle of a divorce, a four-year-old at my side, living with my mother at age 40, sharing my bedroom and bed with my son. All I knew was, "What's due tomorrow?" I couldn't think about or have time for anything else. Things were moving very quickly, and my head was swirling with information and anticipation. I was filled with anxiety to "get the grades" and secure my position as the head of household, bringing home the bacon and taking on my new role as a nurse.

As a child, I wanted to be a doctor, a veterinarian, a stewardess and business owner all at the same time. In high school I was a cheerleader, encouraging and believing in the ability of others. As I grew older, I got married and inherited my husband's family. I eventually cared for his mother who died of cancer and his grandmothers, one who lived with us. It was during that time I immersed myself in health and nutrition and was inspired by the wisdom of shared stories and remedies discovered. I treasured that experience. In spite of the challenges and heartache, there was laughter and joy. Imagine living with and caring for an 87-year-old and a toddler under the same roof. So when faced with a decision of what to do after my divorce, nursing was the choice for me.

School doesn't prepare you to be a nurse, well not entirely that is. Nursing, in the hospital, takes so much multitasking. Typically, I will have three to four patients at a time. Our model is patient-centered care, which means you do all of it. One might have the same patients for days in a row, but nothing is the same from shift to shift. In the hospital, it takes just a split second to go from smooth and structured to critical and chaotic. A nurse has a set of patients with orders to follow and fulfill, but something as simple as giving medications can turn complicated. The patient may have to go to the bathroom, feel nauseous, be in pain, or need an IV site changed. These are the real-world scenarios that are not experienced or taught in classrooms and simulation labs. Additional interruptions to the flow of nursing care are: procedures, tests, consults with physical and occupational therapists, wound specialists, nutritionists, social workers, speech and respiratory therapists, family members, doctors rounding, doctors calling to give phone instructions, secretaries calling informing of appointments and transportation needs. These necessitate time for communication and physically moving people who can't move themselves. As a nurse, you are struggling to find assistance from any available staff when you need it. One can never count on a timeline. Scheduled breaks and lunch times? Forget it. I've gone eight hours in a 12-hour shift before eating or going to the bathroom. (I've joked about inserting a catheter and rigging up an IV bag with a long straw.) It's a fact. There is a huge burnout factor in the field of nursing, which contributes to the current shortage of nurses. Within the first three years of clinical practice, up to 50% of new nurses either change positions or leave nursing completely.

Giving quality care is physically challenging and exhausting, yet it can be very rewarding. It's gratifying to get a smile, a few kind words and a hug from a patient. Nurses hold their hand, cry with them, laugh with them, knowing that you may be the ONLY person in their life that is there at that moment caring for them. It's gratifying to share information that enables patients to make medical and health choices that are right for them. It's gratifying to be the safety net when things go south, being the eyes and ears and reacting in the nick of time, advocating for patients, making sure their wishes are honored and empowering them to make healthful changes after leaving the hospital. These are the interactions I love, and they can leave me feeling like I'm floating on cloud nine. If only that feeling would linger.

Well, on this particular day, it didn't. In nursing terms, floating means to be assigned to another floor for your shift. And let me tell you, this is no zen moment for most nurses. Technically, your nursing care is the same: get a report, check orders, pass medications, facilitate the journey for each patient that day. However, each floor has a different specialty and a different and often unfamiliar staff. Things are just… well... different.

It was my turn to float. The morning had been routine and rather uneventful. Little did I know that afternoon would be anything but ordinary. Sometimes it seems as though there is a bewitching hour called "shift change," when everything crazy happens at the same time. It happened that afternoon. Three out of four of my patients developed complications simultaneously. Two were experiencing chest pain, and one was about to turn blue with an oxygen saturation as low as 40 for a brief moment (a pulse oximetry reading of less than 88 is considered low). All of them needed my immediate attention. All of them needed STAT vitals, STAT EKG's and their medical teams called. And to make matters worse, each patient had a different team to notify. There were only two EKG machines available, and I didn't have the code to take out the medications quickly. I remember literally stumbling out of the med room, laughing and crying at the same time. With tears rolling down my cheeks, I recall thinking, "What the X&?* do I do?!!!! AUGGGHHHH." All I wanted to do was to run away and cry. As I emerged out the med room, I heard the voice inside say, "Come on, Monica. Get it together. You can DO THIS! You've GOT TO DO THIS!!!"

Standing at the nurse's station, I took a deep breath and wiped my eyes. Something clicked, and I jumped into action. I instructed the secretary to call the Rapid Response Team for the respiratory patient and requested the charge and other nurses' involvement. It's amazing how the focus shifts with each staff member playing their part, switching gears as though on emergency autopilot. Everyone came together, and in spite of the initial confusion, systematically each patient was well attended. I can still feel my heart pounding and hear the wheels turning in my brain, wondering if I had done all I could and thinking, "Had I given the proper nursing care, followed the procedures correctly and given all the correct information?" Of course, self-doubt crept in. I had been responsible for four patients, three of them had major crises at the same time. The fact that not one patient was transferred to the ICU and all were stable by the end of my shift was a miracle in itself. When I walked off that ward at the end of the day, I was spent. My nerves were shot. The events played over and over in my mind. "What if I had done this or that. Would it have made a difference? Could any of this have been avoided? What if someone had died?" These self-talk questions were agonizing. I never thought nursing would be like this or that I would feel this way about a job I loved. This was a pivotal point in my career. I honestly wanted to quit. I think every nurse has had those thoughts at one time or another, but this event was a game changer if there ever was one. I went home and proceeded to cry myself to sleep.

When I woke up the next morning, I still wanted to quit. I was even calculating what I could do and seriously making an exit plan. It wasn't just that I was exhausted and stressed out. It was the sobering realization that I was responsible for people's lives, a responsibility that can't be taken lightly. And one that, at that moment, I wasn't sure I could live up to. Although I hadn't witnessed death that day, I had in the past and was again living through sleepless nights because of it.

I am so thankful for the hugs, compassion and the gratitude of others. It's what saved me from quitting. When I shared the events and my feelings with a fellow nurse about that traumatic day, she hugged me and said, "Ah, I'm so sorry. But you are a great nurse. Don't forget all the patients you've helped and how special you make them feel." She mentioned a particular patient we had cared for and how I had intervened on her behalf, which resulted in a heartfelt positive outcome for both the patient and this nurse.

The memory of that day, her gratitude, understanding, compassion, warm heart and embracing hug eased my self-doubt and reminded me of what I loved about nursing. There are many aspects and dimensions of nursing. Besides the physical pressures, there are the emotional dilemmas to overcome. We are, mind you, the buffer, the "Rock "and "Hope" for the sick and frail we care for. For instance, how do you go from stressed and almost annoyed to heart-centered and being able to provide a calm atmosphere of respect and dignity for your patients? I was caring for a complicated patient, lying in a pool of diarrhea, who was unable to move and needed to be cleaned up every hour, which was the least of his problems that day. I had a full patient load, and the staff was stretched. Every time I saw his call light go on, I cringed, thinking of the time and effort I would have to expend and of all the things I was getting behind in. There I went again, making my rounds, in search of a staff member with time to assist me. Then I saw how vulnerable and anxious he was. I thought, "What if this was my dad who was in this situation? Or what if it were me?" It's those thoughts that incite how thankful I was to be there. I took a couple of deep breaths and with intention, cleared my mind with a quick meditation. I held his hand and said, "We will get through this together."

In this business, you need to make lemonade out of lemons. It is with kindness and respect, humor at times, and interesting and sometimes colorful conversation that will go a long way to ease the tension, take the focus off the task at hand and normalize the activity, to a degree anyway. His gratitude touched my heart, and I knew this is why I am here, to serve my patients. Did it lessen my exhaustion or frustration and the need to recoup? No. But I recognized that self-care is so important and being grateful for our blessings is healing in itself.

I believe our bodies are designed to heal themselves if given what they need, a truth I learned and embraced before my nursing career. And as Florence Nightingale said, "What nursing has to do... is to put the patient in the best condition for nature to act upon him." When it comes right down to it, it's up to each and every one of us. We have to intrinsically have the desire to create wellness in our lives and the mindset to do it. I believe gratitude plays a huge role in that transformation.

It takes a lot of hard work to get well. I know that first hand. Getting injured in 2014 and recovering for ten months gave me time to ponder what type of nurse I wanted to be, to look at nursing from a different perspective and live in gratitude. I learned to appreciate all the little things like walking and reaching and bending without pain. During my recovery, I went to physical therapy and acupuncture sessions twice a week for months and forced myself to do my assigned exercises. I ate healthily, took supplements, herbs, and used essential oils. I took the time to implement and practice meditation, visualization, breathing and then yoga as I started to get better. This was an intentional mind shift. I learned how powerful thought really is and that being grateful instills the feelings that shift our thoughts. These techniques worked for me and are evidenced-based. It was after this injury that I became a student of Healing Touch (an energy therapy that is heart-centered and an intentional caring-healing modality.) I started applying this to my nursing practice, as well as range of motion and sharing these holistic techniques to as many patients who are interested.

Patients get burnt out, too, like my mother-in-law did. I wanted to help her. I wanted her to live, to see her grandson be born. I tried everything I could think of to build her strength, keep her spirits high and stay alive. But in the end, it wasn't my decision. She was tired of fighting the battle and told me she was done. It was hard to let go, but I understand how humbling it is to be a part of that whole process.

I wish I would have known then what I know now to help my mother-in-law. I would share with her what I've learned since she passed and what I do with my patients. There is nothing more powerful than our thoughts. What we think about, we bring about. That when regret and negative thought is replaced with gratitude and thankfulness, new doors open. That identifying and resonating with the feeling of joy and peace, by thinking more on those thoughts, these will manifest positive outcomes. That when we intentionally seek these thoughts and the feelings of gratitude, it creates a shift in our mindset. Our mindset plays a huge role in our health, our healing, and our relationships.

Life is full of stress and nursing is certainly one example where that holds true. Stress affects our health and body, our thoughts and feelings and our behavior. From nurses to patients, everyone benefits in life when stress is addressed, managed, reduced and/or relieved. There are many ways people can choose to deal with it. Sometimes shouting expletives, pulling out hair or having a glass of wine (or four) may or may not relieve tensions. However, I have found that the most profound way of dealing with my stress and burnout is through being thankful and grateful. Every day I write affirmations in my journal and what I am grateful for. I practice meditation and deep breathing, pray, and do yoga. This creates a powerfully positive shift in my attitude which gives me strength during strenuous times. It truly is healing. And by sharing this with my patients and the world, I know I am changing lives. I am making a difference.

Monica Andrusko RN, BSN, CNHP

Monica Andrusko, RN, had a glass half-full to overflowing mindset from the time she was a child and teenage cheerleader. Along with compassionate quality nursing care, she strives to help people discover their healing potential and find positivity and passion in their life's journey. As a medical/surgical nurse in a hospital setting for the last nine years, Monica seeks opportunities to share holistic means of healthcare. As a student of Healing Touch, she integrates this therapy when time and interest allows. Monica has studied multiple healing modalities including Contact Reflexology, iridology, essential oils, and energy medicine. She is a Certified Natural Health Professional and is certified in Aromatouch. She has Bachelors of Science degrees in Nursing and Marketing. A native Oregonian, Monica has lived in the Willamette Valley, Southern, and Eastern Oregon and currently resides in Portland with her teenage son. She loves to travel, explore nature in the Pacific Northwest and beyond, cook, garden and have fun with friends and family. Monica's aspirations center on helping people be their best, regain their health, aim for wellness and have a renewed look on life.

www.monicasandrusko.com

monica@monicasandrusko.com

"Never doubt that a small group of thoughtful committed citizens can change the world; indeed, it is the only thing that ever has."

—Margaret Mead

A NURSE PIONEER SHARES HER STORY OF TRANSFORMATION

GAIL JETT, RN, MSN, FNP,

WHNP-BC, AHN-BC, EEM-AP, LMT, RMT

have always been a pioneer, eager to try something different, and perhaps not necessarily mainstream. As a child growing up on a small ranch in rural San Diego county in California, I learned many valuable life lessons, as well as self-reliance. These lessons followed me into my career choice of nursing. Sometimes, a profound event shapes or changes a career choice forever. Perhaps this occurs by shaking the very foundations of what one thought, believed, or was told and had been practicing. A life-altering event can cause one to question one's current, accepted paradigm deeply. I had one of those life-changing events. This is my story.

I always wanted to be a teacher. My parents were both teachers, and they inspired me. They were dedicated to their students, and highly respected, often having students come back to them years later to tell them how my parents' teaching affected their lives in powerful and positive ways. I remember both of them hovering over student homework every evening, and on weekends, putting in lots of time after the school day was over. I felt sure this was the direction I wanted my life to go as well. However, my parents being the wise souls they were, gently, firmly and knowingly nudged me towards the nursing profession as it had the potential for better pay and job security for women than teaching did at that time. Interestingly, it was a profession for which I found a new love and a profound respect. Two years after receiving my RN at the age of 21, a physician employer mentioned the life changing words, "Nurse Practitioner." While I had no idea what those words really meant, or what they actually represented, they resonated with something deep inside my core, so I began to research this new concept in nursing.

The first Nurse Practitioner program in the United States began in 1965 in Colorado, created by Dr. Loretta Ford. Approximately ten years later, one of the first university-based Nurse Practitioner programs in California began at Sonoma State University. As this was pre-Internet, I did library research, applied to the program, and promptly moved from San Diego County in California where I had grown up, to Rohnert Park in Northern California, home of Sonoma State University. While I had not yet been accepted, I moved there just knowing I would be accepted into the program!

There are no coincidences, and I received my acceptance letter to the program. Eagerly anticipating what I would learn, I threw myself wholeheartedly into the program, working nights and evenings while carrying a full-time credit load. This course load was daunting, and I found myself dancing with uncertainty over whether I would fully be able to function in this expanded practice role in nursing. However, within the first few years after graduation in 1980, I found myself becoming increasingly secure in my new role; all the while continuing to research what I didn't know, and asking questions of those more skilled and polished than I. These early years provided challenges in the form of patients, physicians and other nurses often questioning what I was doing, and whether my practice was legitimate or even legal. I found myself frequently explaining and defending my expanded role, understanding at a deeper level that what I was doing was frequently misunderstood, and sometimes even threatening to certain others in the healthcare professions. I was constantly in a position to either defend, or enlighten others about what I did, and I called upon the grounded research that was available at the time to explain to others my practice parameters. Because of this, I realized that I loved learning, and returned for my Master's in Nursing, this time attending the University of San Diego. Graduating in 1990, I did some teaching in the undergraduate nursing program there, as well as at a local community college where I covered a semester's sabbatical for an instructor. I found that while I loved teaching nursing students, I found myself wanting to teach my patients more preventative health practices, so I did that as well in the form of community-based education.

Changes in the healthcare arena in California as well as in my personal life sent me on a new adventure, leading me to Idaho in 1996. While living and working there, I had the opportunity to precept Nurse Practitioner students in a family practice setting. A serendipitous chat with their instructor one day caused me to send resumes to Oregon, as many parts of the state's Nurse Practice Act and regulations for Nurse Practitioners also resonated with me. Of course, the beautiful outdoors and recreational activities struck a chord as well. I received an offer of a job with a large Ob/ Gyn practice, and soon found myself a resident of Oregon, where I have lived since 1999.

Working in a variety of nursing employment settings served to give me perspective, as well as contributing to a growing restlessness inside myself, a recognition that something within my professional practice settings and goals for my patients was still missing. My early Nurse Practitioner program training had emphasized the importance of health maintenance, but also preventative health practices. I enthusiastically studied, and taught my patients the best health practices based on what I knew, staying current with professional recommendations while still wondering what I could do better. I often questioned the wisdom of practicing a model of "one size fits all" in terms of treatment of clients, recognizing that each of us is different. In addition, it was a deep knowing, a recognition that our healthcare system and its providers, often tended to rely on prescribing medicines to control symptoms, rather than really trying to get to the root cause of the symptoms themselves. Obviously, there were several reasons for this which could include time available for client visits, standards of care, practice parameters, client expectations, and providers' philosophies. Like other providers caring for our clients, I ordered the requisite studies, such as imaging and laboratory testing, which were sometimes helpful, but often lacking in big picture explanations or even answers; leaving more unanswered questions for my clients, and myself as to what was really going on.

One day, on a cold, dreary day in October of 2007, I was going through a stack of junk mail, shredding much of it. I picked up a postcard with a caption that said something to the effect of "did I want to increase my energy?" On that particular day, I was feeling the effects of the bleak weather, so I yawned and started to just put the postcard in the shredder. In an instant, it was as if something grasped my arm, stopping me from putting the postcard into the intake slot. I re-examined it and noticed that I could get nursing continuing education credits for this workshop, a requirement for my nursing license renewal. I glanced at it further and saw that the workshop was being held in Seattle, a six-hour drive north. The workshop was being presented by a woman named Donna Eden, and her husband, David Feinstein. These presenters were both unfamiliar to me, but since I needed the continuing education hours, and the workshop was relatively close in terms of distance, I decided to sign up for it.

I asked a friend if she wanted to ride up with me, and we left on the Friday of the workshop and headed to Seattle. We arrived at the hotel, frazzled and tired after nearly a seven-hour drive ending with rush hour traffic on a Friday evening in Seattle. By the time we got checked into the hotel the workshop had already started, so we had decided to get dinner and call it an early night. This turned out to be a big mistake on my part, as I was to learn the next day.

Saturday, the second day of the workshop, was magical and transformational. Donna Eden taught and had us practice different techniques of something she called "energy medicine" which physically felt amazing, and left me with more questions than answers. I came away from it, after experiencing this, wanting to know more and to understand exactly what we had done. I regretted my decision the evening before not to attend, wondering what pearls of wisdom I had missed! I remember looking in the mirror while brushing my teeth, telling myself I wanted to learn more about this and knowing deep inside that my life was about to change forever in a profound way.

The next day, Donna's husband, David Feinstein, a published, bright and well-spoken psychologist, gave an amazing workshop on EFT, or Emotional Freedom Tapping. His presentation included PET scans of the brain, comparing images after patients had either done the EFT techniques or used benzodiazepines for anxiety. The results were truly significant, as the images showing the areas in the brain affected by the EFT were much larger than the area affected by the benzodiazepines. I was sold right there! The evidence he presented convinced me that this was an important path to patients' healing that I needed to explore further.

I began the Eden Energy Medicine Certification program in 2008, completed the clinical practicum, and all the advanced classes. I love this work and am now on the program's faculty. My life has become transformed as a result of this whole experience. Donna Eden, able to see the Human Energy Field, had healed herself from several significant health problems, the most serious being multiple sclerosis which at the time had not been helped by conventional medical care. A vibrant, enthusiastic woman of boundless energy, she was able to help develop a program that would allow its students to use her techniques to help balance others' energies, as well as their own. Based in part on ancient Chinese Medicine as well as other modalities, the training addresses energetic imbalances with a goal of attaining a mastery of techniques designed to help people address their own energy imbalances. I was able to integrate these techniques into my conventional practice of women's health care in a busy Ob/Gyn practice, recognizing that the core issue I had been looking for in terms of true preventative health was finally becoming clear to me.

The Human Energy Field exists, has been scientifically studied, and is the basis for many ancient healing modalities, as well as modern practices. Martha Rogers introduced it into nursing education in 1970 with her theory of the Science of Unitary Human Beings, which provides a framework and explanation for energy-based modalities. The nursing profession itself lists Disturbed Energy Field as a nursing diagnosis. Chinese medicine, as well as other modalities, believes that disease first manifests as a disturbance in the energy field, and that through identification and correction of the disturbance, disease itself may be avoided, improved, or even corrected in the physical body. The study of Quantum Physics also provides intriguing insights into the nature and behavior of subtle energies and sub-atomic particles. One other critical component in healing the body and the mind is also addressing emotions and spirit, as all of these interact together. Eden Energy Medicine provides a methodology to help balance these elements, as well as an effective way to reprogram subtle energies that develop and persist as suboptimal habits, even when they are not beneficial for our well-being. This, then, is the true preventative foundation that I had found myself searching for! While nutrition, exercise, rest, and meditation are also key components, they must be partnered with a balanced energy field in order to promote health. I continue to research and share the gold standard modern scientific evidence that helps to explain how energy healing modalities work in the classes that I teach.

The last ten years of my nursing career have been reshaped and forever altered by Energy Medicine. My worldview of healthcare has changed and expanded too, with the understanding that people can learn easy, powerful tools to help them attain their health goals. I have watched many clients adopt these practices and have witnessed truly amazing healing occur. I am so humbled by this; what a privilege to be able to participate!! While somewhat daunting, I made the decision in October of 2016 to step away from conventional healthcare to focus solely on my business; doing what I have come to believe is truly preventative healthcare. I am doing this through health coaching, teaching and the practice of energy medicine. As I have seen the improvements in my own life, my goal is to share this with as many people as possible. Once more, I am using my pioneering spirit to act as a change agent in an attempt to help others understand and utilize the innate healing ability of their own bodies. In doing this, it challenges them to own their own power through an increasing understanding of the importance of partnering with themselves as well as their healthcare providers to improve their health and wellbeing. And I for one, commit to continuing to be a lifelong student of this work.

Gail Jett, RN, MSN, FNP, WHNP-BC, AHN-BC, EEM-AP, LMT, RMT

Gail Jett received her RN in 1974 and went on to obtain a BSN and Family Nurse Practitioner Certification in 1980 from Sonoma State University. In 1990, she received her Master's in Family Health Nursing and a Women's Health Nurse Practitioner in 2001. Gail became an Advanced Holistic Nurse in 2009 and is currently pursuing her doctorate in Holistic Medical and Counseling Intuition. She is also a Licensed Massage Therapist and Reiki Master. Her 43-year nursing career has led her through three states and a variety of employment positions, all of which have contributed to who she is today. For the last ten years, Gail's passion has been to share the wisdom and empowerment of Energy Medicine, particularly with other healthcare professionals. She believes that nurses, in particular, are the fundamental backbone of healthcare and can be powerful change agents. An understanding of the scientific evidence supporting energy healing modalities can help bring this needed modality into mainstream healthcare. Gail is married and shares her home with her husband, four cats, and one dog. Her hobbies include riding motorcycles, camping, hiking, knitting, and reading.

www.advancedhealingenergetics.com

gailjett53@gmail.com

"The planet does not need more successful people. The planet desperately needs more peacemakers, healers, restorers, storytellers, and lovers of all kinds."

—Dalai Lama

Journey Towards Gratitude

MAURA EGAN, RN

A s I gazed out the plane window at the snow-covered Carpathian Mountains of Romania, I worried I had gotten in way over my head. What was I doing, traveling 6,000 miles away from my sweet life, flying into a region perilously close to the 1991 Persian Gulf War? I became aware of the plight of the Romanian orphans, casualties left by a tyrant. The scenes on television, the newspaper stories of these 200,000 children, abandoned in orphanages, some even with parents and families, were heartbreaking!

The awareness of this tragedy coincided with a growing, nagging little voice inside my head, urging me to "do something productive with your life." Sure, I had raised two incredible sons and one amazing daughter in the small community of Cottage Grove, Oregon. I enjoyed a satisfying job in the local hospital's operating room and had a loving partner. Weekends found me coaching one of my children's soccer teams, refereeing other games and sailing my beloved sailboat on the beautiful local lakes. In other words, life was good. But, something was missing. I felt like I had skills learned over many years of nursing and yearned to share them with others. When the call came for volunteers to join an international medical team overseas, I applied, feeling this was my chance to step up and take action. Being chosen from many qualified applicants filled me with excitement and gratitude. Our team of eleven nurses, doctors, and translators would make up the first team to enter Romania in over a decade. Our mission was performing corrective eye surgery on these forgotten, troubled little citizens.

How had so many ended up there? I learned that during the decades-long regimen of the Romanian dictator Nicholas Ceausescu, there was virtually no money allocated to healthcare or medical technology (think the 1940s) nor any funds for the basic care of children housed in the state-run orphanages. These children were turned over by their own parents, who were too poor to care for them. Ceausescu's maniacal quest for a national labor pool of 30 million people by the century's end meant that all forms of birth control and abortions were banned. To guard against self-terminated pregnancies by desperate women, Ceausescu's "baby police" tested thousands of female workers monthly to detect and track each pregnancy. Intrusion on a huge scale by the state into family planning, left destitute and desperate families handing over their children to state- sponsored homes, hoping and believing the state would look after them.

As the number of children increased, so did the squalid and Dickensian conditions they now resided in. A lack of qualified caregivers, personnel, and maintenance workers left a horrific vacuum in the lives of these dependent children. On our TV screens, we saw decrepit turn of the century buildings lacking basics like central heating, hot water, and plumbing. Flush toilets, forget it! After we had arrived, we realized that the ice-covered holes out in the courtyards were sometimes the only bathing areas these kids had. Apparently, it had been difficult to convince morally-suited caregivers to stay and care for the children. One couldn't blame these staffers. It was a huge challenge for them even to take care of and feed their own families while trying to survive the brutal regime in which they existed. Many good Romanians and there were many, had to shut their eyes to other problems. Once you understood that a single matron or caregiver would be responsible for feeding, dressing, and bathing perhaps 50 children apiece, you knew in your heart that replacing judgment with gratitude was the right thing to do.

Although many details related to our mission were still being negotiated even as we arrived in a January blizzard, we all agreed, that improvising would be paramount to our success. We would start at the frozen airport unloading terminal, taking note of the supplies and donated equipment that generous hospitals and charitable donors had gifted us. There were portable OR lights, some special OR tables, two anesthesia machines, cardiac monitors, suction machines and much more.

Driving into the city, it became apparent just how challenging this would be. Glimpses through the fogged-up windows of our van revealed the after-effects of the heavy winter blizzard. Instead of seeing snow plows clearing the streets, we saw rows of women, older women, babushkas, and grandmothers pushing snow with plywood squares nailed onto long boards, their version of homemade snow shovels.

Once we arrived at our accommodations, it became clear how this mission would unfold amidst power outages, unreliable heat, long hours, and hard work. Incredible sadness, and yet, a sense of increasing gratitude for this opportunity to serve others much less fortunate took root.

In the days to come, we would feel lucky if we could start our days with 30 minutes of hot water. Before our first meal and meeting the Romanian team, I had apprehension about how they would view us. Would they view us as interlopers or team members? Nothing, however, could have prepared us for the genuine hospitality and gratitude shown us as we entered a hall for our first meal with the nurses, doctors, and administrators on their team. The meal consisted of hard-boiled eggs, yogurt, a soft white cheese and a grayish wiggly aspic with horse meat! Our hosts shared this with great pride and generosity, a humble gesture that filled our hearts with profound thanks because we were aware of the food shortages.

I began to appreciate the little things of daily life I had taken for granted back home, like having a hot shower and a delicious breakfast before heading off to my day. It was becoming clear we were in a land where comforts, ideas, and feelings had been dominated by laws - strict and arcane.

The hospital was located in a district that had once been an international beauty, described as "the little Paris of the East." As a matter of fact, the actual building we worked in was an 110-year-old former bank - an older version of a once beautiful Parisian model, now with dull marble stairs, creaky chairs, and worn wooden banisters.

Before we could get down to operating on our little patients, we would meet up with the staff who did the pre-op selection process in the clinics and then visit a few of the orphanages. These visits would be grueling - mentally, emotionally, and physically. This task became enormously easier once we had the opportunity to meet, among many, the nuns from Mother Teresa's order. Clad in their white and blue-trimmed habits, these women were the embodiment of compassion, dedication, and selflessness. They introduced us to the little ones - Florentina, Angelina, Nicoletta and many others, who by and large, sat still, quietly staring and observing us from their drab white metal crib-like beds.

The sad reality was many of these kids had never been picked up, never really cuddled, never truly played with like normal children until recently. My maternal heart stirred at the sight of children pulling away from us in fear or banging their heads on the bed railings. Knowing they would now have an opportunity for a changed destiny, a life filled with potential and love, thrilled me to my core.

The streamlined process of preparing the children involved not only the surgical aspects but copious amounts of soothing words, warm, gentle hugs, stuffed animals and singing many off-key rhymes. We held them snugly in our laps, wrapped in warm blankets, as our adept anesthesiologist drifted them off to sleep and a bright new future. Prior to bringing them into the rooms, we'd set up, as best we could, an efficient, smooth-running semblance of a surgery suite.

We were figuring out how to use and reuse items like blood pressure cuffs, EKG pads and sterile gloves, items that are currently for single patient use and are plentiful in the U.S. I noticed the surgeons and staff would wash their hands at the scrub sinks then pour that old-fashioned orange antiseptic, Methiolate, all over their hands then proceed gloveless into the operating room. Sterile gloves were not as readily available as at home.

What essentials do we have in an America operating room besides gloves, that weren't found in the hospital there? Think for a moment how crucial an inexhaustible supply of oxygen would be. There was a fellow in charge of their few tanks of O2, stationed on the ground floor in a courtyard, yelling up three floors to an open window to inform us "only 30 minutes of oxygen left." We'd scramble to finish up ongoing cases, careful to only use our small portable tanks if necessary. It was mind-boggling, to say the least. At home, we had models of efficiency, standards of care, sterility, and modern medicine at our fingertips. Here, in Romania, the inefficient and sordid had ruled healthcare, up until this period in their history. At home in Oregon, it was just taken for granted we would use sterile packs of supplies for each surgery, packs of suture or suction tubing, used once and discarded. Not so in Bucharest, in an operating room that resembled something from the '40s or '50s. The rumbling, creaky, old ornately gated elevators in the former bank building also might not be working at the exact moment we would need one. Upon completing a surgery and starting to transfer these little patients two stories below to the recovery room, we'd discover the "no service" sign hung out. We'd now resort to Plan B and prepare to carry them down the stairwell together, a nurse, an anesthesiologist, and a translator, huddled together, anxious, and acutely aware of our precious cargo.

The overall brainstorming and improvising in difficult situations allowed me to see I could contribute my own set of individual skills as both a nurse and a woman. When faced with these obstacles, we worked harder, pushed harder and acknowledged the fact that as a team, we were a force of good in the world. So it was very uplifting to experience the Romanian doctors and nurses also coming together to learn from us. They were curious and inquisitive from the beginning about how to operate our equipment, open to questioning our techniques and our teamwork. The competency of our host team was compelling and inspiring to us all. The impact we were having on the lives of these children was motivation enough for me. Knowing that time zones away, these procedures would be considered routine, matter-of-fact day surgeries was a stark reminder that as Americans, we should be deeply grateful.

It takes only a compassionate heart and a willingness to listen to affect a change in the world. Volunteering for this mission launched me on a new career path in disaster relief nursing for the next 25 years. This aspect of my nursing livelihood has enabled me to enter a cross-cultural realm where I continue to collaborate with and be inspired by strong male and female nurses. My day-to-day nursing path has been enriched beyond measure as a result of my overseas experiences and adventures.

As that plane first touched down in Romania 25 years ago, I emerged an anxious, unsure neophyte. I boarded that plane home a changed human being. As painful and challenging as that trip was, a major shift occurred. A tsunami of gratitude washed over me. I learned to sincerely appreciate every small aspect of pulling off "minor miracles" with simple, humble, hard work side by side with complete strangers, now friends.

Maura Egan, RN

With three generations of nurses running in her veins, Maura has relished 46 years as an operating room nurse and a team member on disaster relief missions, combining her wanderlust with service to humanity. She has worked and traveled in different countries in Central America, South America, Eastern Europe and right here in the United States after Hurricane Katrina.

When home in Eugene, Oregon, she loves tending her garden, maintaining her home, spending time outdoors in nature, and romping around the state with her children and grandchildren. She practices Vipassana Insight Meditation to help her observe life in an expansive and positive light. Believing in the power of self-healing, Maura incorporates Therapeutic Touch on her patients. She also loves using aromatherapy on her family, friends, herself, even occasionally, her two feline housemates, Pudding and Duke.

pacificgrace3@aol.com

"When an illness is a part of your spiritual journey, no medical intervention can heal you until your spirit has begun to make the changes that the illness was designed to inspire."

—Caroline Myss

Stoking the Fires of Change

JESS YOUNG, RN, BSN

While on The Big Island of Hawaii, a sage elder gifted me with the story of the Phoenix. According to the elder's lineage, the Phoenix, indeed, was a real bird that existed during the Jurassic period. The Phoenix was the fiercest bird to ever live, slightly larger in size than the bald eagle, with striking plumage painted in every color of the rainbow. The story goes that the shell of the Phoenix egg was thicker than a typical eggshell; it was so dense that the baby Phoenix could not peck its way through without some assistance. Being that nature is a reflection of perfect balance, which unfailingly supports life, there was a natural solution to this challenge. The mother bird would instinctively lay her eggs in an area that was prone to forest fires. In divine timing, the baby Phoenix would be on the precipice of hatching just as the forest fire began raging. The heat from the flames would assist in the weakening of the eggshell so that the baby bird could peck through its first, earthly challenge and set itself free. And so, as depicted throughout history, the Phoenix could be seen triumphantly flying up and out of the flames--it is a universal symbol of life, death, and rebirth.

I continue to reflect on the symbolism that the auspicious Phoenix represents in my life. The most obvious representation exists in my career as a registered nurse; I have seen many extreme manifestations along the dis-ease spectrum in the ten years that I have practiced nursing. As a nursing student, I had the honor to stare in wonder down into an ice-filled chest cavity during open-heart surgery. The surgeon, perhaps intuiting my unconscious need to broaden my appreciation for life, allowed me to hold the man's heart in my hand. Meanwhile, his blood circulated, --lub-dub, lub-dub-- with the help of a machine, which mimicked the pumping of the heart. I could see and hear his lungs inflating and deflating in his chest as the machine "inhaled" and "exhaled" for nearly eight hours that day. This profound experience in the operating room was as much a personal rite of passage as it was a professional one. My perception of life and death was forever changed that day, as the fine line that exists between the two realities was now more tangible to me.

In the first hour of my first job as a licensed nurse, I witnessed the grace of a soul transitioning from the cancer-riddled body of a Vietnam Veteran. The memory of the post-mortem care that I provided is something that will stick with me until my earthly passing. At twenty-three, my prior life experience paled in comparison to the depth of these two instances. In hindsight, I see where creating time and space to reflect and express my feelings would have been incredibly beneficial for my emotional, physical and spiritual well-being. Alas, self-care and healthy coping strategies were not part of the nursing school curriculum.

I liken myself to the baby Phoenix in these moments. A fledgling nurse fresh out of the comfort and safety of school, my career's first trial by fire was in the intensity and rawness of each pivotal experience and in the choice to do whatever it took to keep flying. On an unrealized mission to witness extreme dis-ease, I was drawn to explore oncology further and became certified to administer chemotherapy. Eventually, I sharpened my ability to ride the thermals between life and death as a guide for those in need. Supporting others through tragic times came naturally to me, and I began to funnel all of my energy into my work without saving some for myself. My patient's family members would ask, "Isn't there something more we could be doing to palliate the symptoms? Aren't there natural remedies that could augment the chemotherapy? What about acupuncture?" My barren holistic toolbox was unequipped to answer their questions; I humbly told them that I was not sure and to consult the physician. My twelve-hour shifts began to melt together, and by the fourth day, I felt half-alive, with my neck and shoulders bound-up into one, giant knot of stress. I was a textbook example of what it means to be "selfless." Self-less, a word used throughout my nursing program by multiple instructors; a word used to describe a worthy characteristic of a good nurse. Merriam-Webster defines selfless as: "Having no concern for self."

I never considered that there was anything wrong with this picture of the medical status quo, let alone that there was anything I could do to improve conditions. On some level, though, I knew that I needed a change, so I moved west to Portland, Oregon. I was magnetized to a new specialty-- child/adolescent and adult inpatient behavioral health. Here, I witnessed the thin veil that exists between sanity and psychosis. Working on the psych ward was like walking through a dark, stagnant cloud of angst and emotion. My intention each day was to shine my light into every crevice of the unit and into the hearts of those who were suffering. After each shift, I would leave feeling like I was coated, inside and out, with a toxic residue of something that wasn't mine. This energetic sludge, as unsavory as it was, also served my evolution by awakening my senses to the unseen. As a result, my eyes, heart, and gut began to focus in on what I had not yet fully perceived. Like waking up while in the midst of sleepwalking, I too snapped out of it. Slowly, I tap tap tapped my way out of my shell and set myself free from the all-consuming flames. Suddenly, I began to realize that the "medicine" I practiced was not at all in alignment with my core, soul values or my beliefs about healing.

The Phoenix had begun to take flight, and she began to see the extent of the forest fire down below. Ativan and Valium were being handed out like candy. The food served to the patients was mostly processed or from a can, lending little sustenance for those attempting to heal in body, mind, and spirit. Sugar was the primary drug given to children who were on Adderall for hyperactive behavior. The teenagers proudly took cocktails of medications—antidepressants, anxiolytics, antipsychotics and mood stabilizers. Rather than looking for the root cause of the behavioral disturbance, physicians were quick to give a diagnosis and offer a medication regimen—one prescription fits all! The nurses were themselves unhappy and unbalanced, trapped in the vices of unhealthy habits. It was now clear to me that the sick were leading the sick! The more I opened my eyes, the more in touch I became with my internal reality. The healthcare system disheartened me. My ability to care was exhausted. I had reached a place I thought was impossible for me to reach; I was burned out. Once the Phoenix breaks free from its shell, it doesn't go back into the flames. In search of medicine that heals illness by restoring balance, I quit my job and soared over to another reality. Guided by my heart, I met a naturopathic physician/acupuncturist who was seeking to work with someone like me. We apprenticed each other: as she learned to collaborate with a Western nurse, I drew from her wealth of knowledge on natural remedies, Chinese medicine, homeopathy, acupuncture, and self-care. Together, we served patients with a broad range of diagnoses—from digestive issues, allergies, and chronic fatigue, to women's health, cancer, and depression. After two years of practicing from her lovely home, we outgrew our nest and expanded into a larger one. Now, some twenty integrative practitioners—naturopaths, acupuncturists, massage therapists, chiropractors, and counselors all collaborated to provide holistic care to the larger Portland community. My wings stretched as I grew into my role as the clinic nurse manager, phlebotomy extraordinaire, and practitioner of hydrotherapy and energy medicine.

I was in awe as I witnessed this healthcare utopia: patients receiving care from multiple practitioners, who would meet weekly to discuss the whole person and the best approach for each individual. Glowing patients conveyed feeling fully supported on their paths to wellness; people were actually healing right before my eyes! Eliminating foods that inflame the body healed those with lifelong allergies. Headaches and insomnia went out the door. Women having difficulty conceiving were with child now after taking prescribed Chinese herbs. All of this occurred with a minimal use of pharmaceutical Band-Aids masking the symptoms. Together, patient and provider were getting to the root cause of the dis-ease. Two-hour, in-depth intakes and one-hour follow-up visits were the norm. As much as we loved our patients, our goal was to help them heal and send them on their way. Most major insurance companies covered the care we provided—one of the perks of living in a progressive city, such as Portland. We were blessed to have a billing specialist who knew how to bill and code to suit the requirements of the powers that be.

Perched on a towering tree, the Phoenix was now empowered and rejuvenated. With self-care practices in my holistic toolbox and massage therapists at my fingertips, my stress knots were gone. I had broadened my perspective of what is possible for our healthcare system and for healthcare professionals. From this viewpoint, a message was clear: in order to continue caring for others, I must first care for myself. My energetic chalice must be refilled with all things nourishing: nature, organic food, community, creativity, dance, meditation, and prayer. I was a living example of a word, which I coined: self-full. I was allowing time after work to unwind, exercising, hydrating, eating well, limiting sugar and alcohol--I even kicked my coffee addiction! It felt enlivening to care for my body in this way-- a true act of self-love. Self-full, I was and continue to be.

Now, two years later, I supervise the care provided to beloved elders in a residential care facility, where our mission is to give the residents a sense of purpose in their final years. I have much more stress in my life now and choose to see it as an opportunity to put my practice into action. Admittedly, coffee is back on the scene, in addition to some unhealthy habits, yet I manage to prioritize self-care and fill my life with people and activities that truly nurture my soul. When the job gets tough, I take time to reflect on why I chose to be a nurse in the first place—to be of service. Alas, the proverbial pendulum unfailingly swings in both directions. Days will be stressful, and we will find ourselves in uncomfortable situations. We will forever be finding our balance in every moment. When feeling unbalanced, I find it helpful to ask myself these questions: Am I acting from a place of personal integrity in every moment? Have I honored others through thoughtful and deliberate communication? Have I honored myself by expressing my needs and what I authentically feel in each situation? If not, why and what can I do to change that? Through this practice, I am learning to own my wings, and by doing so, I am showing others that flying out of the flames can be graceful, rather than choosing to feel like I don't have a choice or a voice.

What can I do today to honor my physical body, my emotions, my mind and my spirit? I have found that even a few minutes of quiet time, deep breathing and small doses of movement throughout the day affects all four of these areas of wellness.

Am I showing up for each interaction in my professional and personal life with full presence, compassion, and active listening? If not, then it is time to slow down and prioritize simple human connection.

Am I protecting my free time? My time away from work is sacred. I have learned to say no to certain invitations in order to have strong boundaries around my free time. I try not to have many obligations during my time away from work and prefer to go with the flow and allow myself space to listen to my needs and desires. Resentment surfaces when I neglect my sacred time.

This Phoenix has big visions for shifting the healthcare system. I aspire to implement holistic courses in nursing schools throughout the country so that students are equipped with robust, holistic toolboxes from the start. It is my desire to facilitate tropical retreats for nurses—a haven to come together, decompress, let loose and come back to ourselves so that we can better serve our communities. I dream of hosting national nursing conferences that focus on the shadows of the healthcare system—the major issues that are begging to be looked at. Together, we will inspire solutions to impact change. Finally, it is my dream to integrate my two passions—nursing and dance. A vision came to me while in nursing school: to host radical and creative healing retreats for women with cancer.

Soaring to new heights, the vibrant Phoenix basks in the hope and light of a new day. With patience and vast inspiration, she peers down into a Western healthcare landscape that appears out of balance and engulfed in flames. The fires are fueled by profit and privatization; a world monopolized by pharmaceutical corporations. Unfazed by the scene below, this sovereign Phoenix recognizes that she is a beacon of change. Each flap of her wings encourages the pendulum to swing toward a healthcare system coming into righteous balance. Every thought, word, and action are stoking the fires of change. Although the way may seem uncertain, it is up to us to listen deeply and know that the greater vision of the Phoenix is carried within us all.

Jess Young, RN, BSN

Jess Young is a holistic nurse, teacher, and dancer in Portland, Oregon. Jess is blazing her own trail as a nurse and an artist, creating the life of her dreams. In addition to working full-time as a registered nurse, Jess is growing a global creative initiative for music video production, called Attunement Movement. Inspired to be an agent of change, Jess believes that balance, self-care and the integration of Eastern and Western medicine are the keys to evolving our healthcare system. With a background in oncology, behavioral health, natural medicine, and elder care, Jess is here to educate and empower nurses, patients, and the community-at-large to listen and trust the wisdom of the body, to quiet the mind, to deeply feel and honor one's emotions and to tend to the inner stirrings of the Spirit.

www.JessYoungRN.com

JessYoungRN@gmail.com

"Though nothing can bring back the hour

Of splendour in the grass, of glory in the

flower, We will grieve not, rather find

Strength in what remains behind..."

William Wordsworth

—Ode: *Intimations of Immortality from Recollections of Early Childhood*

I AM A SURVIVOR

DEVORAH (DOROTHY) TAITZ,
RN, BSN

Nurses have one thing in common, the inert passion for helping others. I always wanted to be a nurse, ever since I was eight years old. I used to get allergy shots weekly from Nurse Ethel. I remember telling my mom that I wanted to be a nurse like Ethel. She never knew how special she was to me. I had to go for allergy shots at least twice a week during whole childhood. I would walk in, and she would greet me with a smile. She never hurt me. A shot in the arm twice a week and I never cried, at least I don't remember crying. She would tell me office secrets like when the doctor's wife was having a baby, and how her feet hurt her from standing all day. I remember she had funny looking feet; I know now that they were bunions. She wore a white uniform and a nurse cap. I so wanted to wear one of those, and I did in nursing school and graduation. I became a nurse like Ethel.

I grew up in a loving home, not realizing that I was by default a recipient of IGPTSD (Intergenerational Post

Traumatic Stress Disorder), I somehow learned that we are here to help one another. My parents were Holocaust survivors. They lost most of their family and came to America with nothing but a few acquired belongings. My extended family was small. I had one brother, one grandfather, one aunt, an uncle and several cousins. All of our family, whether they were first cousins or fourth cousins twice removed, were like our immediate family because they were all survivors and the only ones left.

My home was open to all. The little food on our table was there for anyone that walked through our door. My parents gave up their beds for guests and slept on the couch. (You know the one with the plastic covers on it?)

I had two passions, art and nursing. I wanted to be an artist and got accepted to Pratt Institute. My mom, however, didn't want me to be the hippie on the streets in Greenwich Village selling my etchings on the streets back in the 70's. So, I went to Nursing School instead (and still do art on the side). You can view my art on my Facebook Page called Art and Soul by Devorah, my form of therapy.

I became a Pediatric Nurse and worked in the newborn nursery, Pediatrics, Neonatal ICU, and Peds ICU. After marriage and children, I returned to nursing in the school setting. I wanted to be home when my kids were home. Being a school nurse allowed me to be home on holidays, weekends and summers. That was my priority, to be with family, and the little that we had that slowly grew.

Some people think that school nursing is just about pushing bandaids, but that is not the case. For some families, we are the only medical care that a child may receive. In some cases, it's the only love and TLC that a child receives.

After about 20 years of school nursing, major stressors happened in my life. Hurricane Sandy in 2012 hit us hard. We had to move out of our home. A family took us into their home for four months. We never met these people until then. The community united to help one another. I still can't comprehend how I was able to receive these acts of kindness and come away with that without mental damage, although I did have some depression for awhile. Thinking about what my family went through during the war is what kept me going day to day. If they could do it for six years, I could do it for a few months. The outcome was that we became amazing friends with the couple that took us in. The lesson learned is that something always positive comes out of something negative.

After vacationing in Los Angeles in August of 2015, I went for a routine colonoscopy. I received a diagnosis of colon cancer and underwent colon surgery in October of 2015. It took a week or so to research for the top colon surgeon in New York. He removed about 14 inches of my colon. I did not need chemotherapy or radiation. I took a seven-week disability leave of absence from work to recover. My test results came back negative, and I then became an advocate for colonoscopies at work and in my community. I succeeded in getting three women younger and older than myself to go for the procedure. I sent the following statement to everyone I know via social media, emails, and handouts.

I am a Cancer Survivor! Yes, me! The two hardest words I never imagined I would ever say, Thank G-d! For those of you who knew, I want to thank you for your prayers and acts of kindness. Countless people from my community, The Five Towns, Connecticut, New York, Long Island, The

Rockaways, Maryland, New Jersey, Florida, California, Israel, etc., ensured that appropriate prayers were recited and that I had care during the day with food and assistance. Countless people included me on their daily Tehillim(Psalms) lists and inquired about me through different venues. To all these people, my family, my friends, and communities, I can't thank you enough!

Being a nurse, a caregiver most of my life and always trying to help others suddenly changed. I was now the patient, being taken care of, with that disease I always feared.

Well, now I say Boruch Hashem (Thank G-d). Why? Because the same G-d that made me the caregiver also made me the recipient of wondrous acts of kindness from my family, friends, the community, and strangers.

So now I just want to offer free advice. If you are fifty years or older, get your baseline or routine colonoscopies, your PSA's, your Mammos. If you have a family history of any type of cancer, follow up with your doctors. Don't wait. It could save your life! I found out through a routine colonoscopy. Be ahead of the game, and I am here for anyone with questions or stories.

One last thought to leave you with. I learned two slogans in the hospital...Gas is Glorious, and BM's are Beautiful! Boruch Hashem! (Thank G-d).

I was ready to go back to work with a positive attitude. I didn't realize how missed I was at work. I wanted to help anyone and everyone that I could. I wanted to be with my family. I wanted to be the best Bubbie (grandmother), mom and wife that I could. I wanted to look at life with a positive attitude and not sweat the small stuff.

After a few months, I went for an MRI of my body to follow-up to rule out any possible spread of cancer. I then was diagnosed with thyroid cancer, totally unrelated to the colon cancer. If I didn't go for the MRI, I would not have known about it until perhaps too late. I went for a thyroidectomy. At the same time, my daughter had been fighting sinus issues for many months, and she was diagnosed with thyroid cancer at the same time as I was.

It is now about a year later after my colon cancer, ten months since my thyroid cancer. I feel great. My daughter and I are both cancer free and survivors. We helped each other to deal with our stressors.

I continue to be an advocate for colonoscopies and other preventative diagnostics. I came out of this with a positive attitude and am now an advocate for all diagnostic exams, and a natural and healthy lifestyle.

YES! I am an advocate for all cancer screenings! I have a new lease on life and a new and improved attitude. I don't sweat the small stuff. I am here on this earth to do acts of kindness whether it is via nursing or for family or my community. As an Observant Jew, we are obligated to do acts of kindness whether or not they stem from the heart. You never know what goodness may derive out of any random act of kindness. My advice to nurses is to allow others to do acts of kindness for you. Caregivers need to be cradled at times as well, and others feel the need to cradle with their love and kindness. Let others pay it forward. I believe we are here in this world for a reason. We are here to try to make this world a better place for all, one person at a time.

I am truly blessed with a husband, two children, their spouses, and three grandchildren. This is my reward. This is my gratitude. I now live with an attitude of gratitude. I try to emit love, kindness, and compassion to all those that I can. One never knows what outcome one good deed could accomplish.

When I returned to work after my surgery, the amazing welcome back reception from the staff and students touched me deeply. So, I started reaching out to all of them, beyond my required tasks. I observed students more. Why are they really coming to me? Do they actually have a headache or do they need to talk about issues? For some, this may be the only attention and love they may have. I advocated tests to all staff and handed out my "survivor" statement. Staff always came to me before, but now they come just to greet me and maybe ask a question or two.

A couple of weeks ago there was a tragic accident in my school. A young boy was a victim of a TBI (TRAUMATIC BRAIN INJURY). I sent him to the hospital via EMS, where they put him into an induced coma. I decided to visit him on the following Sunday. His mom was there and was delighted to see me. I approached the eight-year-old child and gently touched his arm and whispered his name. He suddenly opened his eyes and looked at me. I smiled and hoped that he was smiling inside. That was all I needed to see to know that he will be all right. I was grateful to God and felt that maybe I did something for his mom and him. They say that the happiest people are those that give the most of themselves. I try to show my kids compassion, love, and kindness. I joke with them when they sit in my chair. I tell them that they too could be a nurse or a doctor. I want them to admire our profession and the beauty and compassion in helping others. I hope that they look up to me like I admired Ethel. I am now Ethel to another generation of children.

Devorah (Dorothy) Taitz, RN, BSN

Devorah, also known as Dorothy, was born in Brooklyn, NY, a first generation American. Growing up in a home of Holocaust Survivors, she knew she was different than her friends and classmates. There had to be something more in life than just living the American dream. Devorah moved to California with her parents and went to Nursing School in Los Angeles. After graduating, Devorah worked as a Nursery, Maternity, Pediatric ICU and NICU nurse. While volunteering in Los Angeles for the Los Angeles Free Clinic, Devorah had the pleasure of meeting some famous Hollywood stars. After meeting her husband, they moved back to New York and started a family.

Devorah returned to working as a nurse in the public-school system. She has two children and three grandchildren and loves every minute of family time. Recovering from two malignant diagnoses, Devorah is back and continues to make this world a better place, one person at a time.

www.facebook.com/Artandsoulbydevorah/

Devorahtaitz@gmail.com

"It is in the quiet crucible of your personal, private sufferings that your noblest dreams are born and God's greatest gifts are given in compensation for what you've been through."

-Wintley Phipps

Igniting Purpose Through Grief

DEONNE WRIGHT, RN

For decades I didn't understand how I knew from the age of three that being a nurse was my life work, but I was crystal clear, and my focus never faltered from achieving that goal. It took half a lifetime for me to understand that Spirit speaks to me through my intuition.

When my mother woke me on a cold, winter, pre-dawn morning to tell me my father's private plane crashed on take-off in the desert near our home, I was twelve years old and sick with a high fever. She answered my questions when I could begin to comprehend. She didn't think he'd survived, and she was proved right. In the days following, my mind grappled with reality, and I gave voice in loud wails to my heart's unanswerable question, "Why?!"

My father and I had an adversarial relationship for as long as I can remember. I was raised by strict, devoutly religious parents. A foundation built on those beliefs allowed no space whatsoever for internal reflection, external exploration, any form of perceived 'worldliness' or questions, and I had many. Because I was twelve years old when he died, I have only my child and pre-teen perspective to rely on regarding our relationship. The healing process afforded me through marriage, motherhood, divorce, multiple losses, spiritual crisis and more than ten years of counseling has given me valuable insight.

Being raised in such a conservative family had many restrictions and limitations. Some were backed by what was claimed to be Scriptural support. Others had no Scriptural connection and made no sense to me. An example was not being able to use hairspray. I was not allowed to cut my hair, so it was past my waist (one of those rules which I was told was Scriptural). New hairs were constantly growing in at the hairline, and I hated how they tickled my face. Hairspray seemed like the obvious solution to me, but my dad said, "If God had wanted you to use hairspray, He'd have grown a can right on your head!" That meant no hairspray for me. It took me longer than I'd have liked to learn how to choose which hill to die on. I was labeled a rebel at a very young age.

It was when I reached my mid-thirties I learned the answer to what I was really asking when I cried out 'Why?!' the day my dad died. In a group counseling session, I suddenly, suffocatingly remembered that two weeks previous to his death I had wished he would die. I believed then it would be easier to live without him than with the pain our relationship was causing me. After his death I took on the responsibility, accountability, and blame, believing it was my punishment. Remembering that helped me understand why pleasing him after his death became an obsession that it never was before.

In 1988 I was a burned-out nurse. I'd re-entered the work force seven years earlier with four young children. I found myself in the same place for the second time in those seven years: exhausted, discouraged with the system, disillusioned and feeling defeated in my goal to significantly impact the lives of my patients. I had lost the deep sense of purpose which had pushed me toward becoming a nurse my whole life. I was desperate to find the clarity I was missing about my calling.

So it was I found myself sitting in a conference room at the hospital where I worked, listening to a presentation in attendance with some fifty other employees. The nurse speaker was extraordinarily dynamic, and it was clear she understood the heart and life of a nurse. But even more, she held out hope for a new way of being with patients that caught my attention.

She shared the story of a twelve-year-old girl whose mother died after a brief time on life support following a motor vehicle accident they were in together. After the mother's death, nursing care intensified toward the daughter. She was told children often take the blame for these events; but if that was true for her, she was assured it was not her fault, and not based in reality. The child cried and confessed that she and her mother had argued immediately prior to the accident and was certain she was at fault. In that single moment, I was transported back in time to the day my father died when I took on the burden of guilt. Through that twelve-year-old girl's story, I was suddenly absolved.

There are moments in our lives when the energy of an old memory or story stored in our visceral body is tapped, and we come undone. That was such a moment for me, and I flew out of the room to avoid embarrassing myself by erupting into sobs right then and there. I found a nearby restroom where I took refuge and could weep without disturbing anyone. Remaining there until I was able to gather myself together, I faced myself in the mirror, knowing something within me had fundamentally shifted. I would never be the same. I'd received the spark of clarity I'd been seeking, my Torch of Purpose was lit, and somehow I would make a difference.

My nursing career has taken me into many environments where I've diagnosed and treated the human response to stress my patients have experienced in their moment(s) of crisis. Stress responses show up in many forms and are experienced in the full expression of the Being – body, mind and spirit. While it is a nurse's job to care for the soul as well as the mind and body, it is also a privilege; for me, it is a calling. A nurse cannot escape being with death, loss, and grief in a forty-plus year career. How s/he learns to deal with it can create a most transcendent experience for patients and families. Death and grief touch the spiritual domains of pain that we tend to avoid. But leaning into that human response to such a deeply profound stress has the potential to heal the soul.

My mother remarried when I was fourteen, and my relationship with my stepfather was far from ideal, even into adulthood. When he died in 2006, I had a complete meltdown but was in confusion about why. I'd never felt close to him, so the grief I was feeling had no explanation in that context. Because I was basically non-functional, I knew I needed help. In spite of counseling three times a week, I was not improving. It was when I began listening to my intuitive self and started using techniques I'd previously learned that I began to get some insight, and shifted out of that disempowering state.

During this time, I was working in Home Care and Hospice, assisting patients and their families through the process of death and dying. Facilitating the dynamics around what matters most, how to communicate about it, how to prioritize it, how to take care of unfinished business, and holding sacred space when a loved one departed the physical body honed my skills. Unfinished business usually wasn't about the physical realm, but more about relationships, reconciliation, meaning and hope. Working with these families in such situations was preparing me to do my own grief work. I was exactly where I needed to be.

As I navigated through my own human response crisis, I received insight gained from working with my hospice patients and families. I'd been spending years doing therapy and spiritual practices in an effort to heal the grief over my father's death. I believed I had accomplished that goal. My patients and their families taught me differently. What they showed me was I first had to heal my relationship with my father before I could heal the grief. I saw that I had put Grief safely away and locked it up. My stepfather's death was the key that unlocked it, allowing it to come crawling back into my consciousness, awareness, and vulnerability. This is an example of the way our subconscious mind hides things from us until we are ready to deal with them.

When I examined where I stood regarding unfinished business with my father, I saw the work I had been doing was healing my relationship with him. Grateful for clarity and understanding, I moved on to embrace and heal the grief. Today I have a song in my heart.

My Torch of Purpose is still fueled by connecting to my vulnerability. Leaning into my own pain feeds the fire that lights the way before me. That helps me keep one foot grounded in being human and the other foot on the healer's path. In that way, I can make a difference for people during their most vulnerable states of human response to stress. When I learn the value of leaning in, I am a contribution. I feel very blessed by my patients and clients who have trusted me in their most vulnerable moments. My gratitude goes to them for teaching me so much.

Deonne Wright, RN

Deonne is a holistic registered nurse who lives in Grants Pass, Oregon. Since leaving the traditional institutional nursing settings, she facilitates transformation for clients in private practice. She obtained her nursing degree from Bakersfield College, and has developed many skills in a varied nursing career. She is a poet, has edited multiple nursing newsletters, and authored the documents that assisted her place of employment achieve national Pathway to Excellence® designation and re-designation. Deonne is a 2007 founding Board member of the Oregon Holistic Nurses Association, and continues to serve on the Board as the volunteer Communications Coordinator, managing the website, blog, facebook page and newsletter. It's a good thing she enjoys a road trip since her dozen grandchildren live from Oregon to Idaho to Texas.

www.deonnesaromablends.com

info@deonnesaromablends.com

"We must learn to regard people less in the light of what they do, or omit to do, and more in the light of what they suffer."

—Dietrich Bonhoeffer

The Wake-Up Call

MAGGIE PERRONE BSN, MA, OCN

I moved from Michigan to Los Angeles to save not only my husband's lagging career, but also in hope of saving my marriage. The year was 2000, a new millennium, and my kids were nine, six and three. With three small children in tow and my 17-year career as a charge nurse in a university health system Level 1 Trauma Center behind me, I found myself in a tony suburb of L.A. It was a place that this Midwestern, Birkenstock-clad girl from the ghetto would have never thought she would find herself.

Sunny Southern California introduced me to a locale, a culture, a way of life and a dress code I never knew existed. We found a lovely, small house, way more than we could afford, but it had to do. I was finally an at-home mom, in a wonderful community, great schools, a great parish to attend and a new beginning. I should have been happy. I should have been content. But I knew, in my bones, this was not the place for me. I tried. I really did. I had great friends and wonderful opportunities. By 2004, I had received a full scholarship to graduate school to study theology and philosophy, a part of myself that I finally had the time, space and a chance to explore. Then it came, the first wake-up call. After three years of struggling, with my husband telling me we were fine and I didn't need to go back to work and a month before I was to start school, he lost his job.

I immediately walked into one of the local hospitals, and two weeks later, I started back in the ER and attended my first graduate-level class. And so it began, the first step in taking back my own life; although I didn't really know it at the time. I worked, two 12-hour shifts in the ER a week, while attending graduate school, taking care of my three kids and watching my marriage fall completely apart as we struggled to maintain that which should have never begun in the first place.

By 2009, I was a newly single mom, with a newly unemployed ex-husband and three kids, one ready to be off to college in the fall. How was I going to do it? I did it the same way I always had: I turned on the back burners and went to work.

A year later, I was overwhelmed with responsibility and work. After earning a master's degree in 2008, I formed my own company, speaking and leading retreats to make a little extra money and feeding my soul a bit in the process. I was working up to five 12- hour shifts a week in the ER to make ends meet. Work-life balance was becoming harder and harder to come by.

As most nurses can relate, and I know we all ask ourselves at times, why do we do it all? More importantly, why do we think we must? For as many reasons as there are nurses. We are trained and then conditioned to act first, prioritize, care for and heal those in pain and misery. Our needs, only at work when we are first starting out, are usually last on our list. The problem is that this tends, over time, to leak out into the rest of our lives and relationships. We tend to take care of everybody else, and we will get to ourselves when…you fill in the blank. And then we realize "everybody else" begins not only to rely on us, but expect us to take care of things, many times those which are not ours, and let's be honest, our ego tends to like it…for a while anyway.

Why do we do it? The best answer I have come up with thus far is this: because we can. We are used to it, used to meeting any challenge with our game face on. We go in—we go deep—we talk about things that nobody dares. We name things that no one wants to name, even those that the events affect the most. We speak about death. We say, "Yes, it was a massive heart attack." We say, "Come right now, drive carefully. Yes, we are sure it is your child." We ask, "Did he hurt you?" and then say, "No, you can't go back. Where are your children? Yes, we will figure out how to keep them safe for you." We hear people say, "I want to die." And we answer, "I can't let you do that, not here, not today, not on my watch and believe me, we will do all we can to get you the help you need."

We can turn on a dime, going from a coffee break to running a full code in 30 seconds or less. Someone needs help, and we are there. Our hand is up before we have even thought about the impact on our already full lives. The question is can we turn it off after work? Can we decrease the dependence on us by those who are more than capable at home? Can we turn it inward to care for ourselves? At what point do we simply have no choice because we are so depleted? What do we sacrifice in our own growth and development by doing so much for all who come into our path? It took a few more years for me to realize how far down the rabbit hole I had actually gone.

It was 2010 when I got to this point, and looking back it was not for the first time. But that is when I began to listen to the wake-up calls, and they were coming in hot— the ones I could no longer ignore. There was the shift in which the homeless man with chronic pancreatitis pulled a knife out because we wouldn't give him pain meds. His amylase and lipase were not abnormal, the hallmark of a pancreatitis flare. As the charge nurse, I had to act. I cleared the ER of visitors and children. I calmly and confidently went to his room and said in my best "mom" voice, "Drop the knife, NOW. No pain meds while you have the knife. And no, there will not be any pain meds unless I have the knife. Drop it on the floor and kick it over to me…RIGHT NOW!" He did. I had no idea what I would have done next if he hadn't.

The final wake-up call was the day I was physically beaten by a patient in the Emergency Department. I was cleaning up a little 93-year-old lady who almost coded after sedation to put her shoulder back in place after a fall. An ambulance had brought me another patient across the hall, but I just couldn't get there at that moment. Next thing I knew the poor cleaning man waved the curtain saying, "Senora! Aqui! Aqui! Mira! Mira!" (Mrs, here, here! Look, look!) I pulled my head around to see the new female patient, all 250 pounds of her, wedged in the corner of the room with drawers upturned, furniture askew and the monitor cords wrapped around her neck. We dropped the 93-year-old patient like a sack of potatoes and flew across the hall.

As I tried to get my fingers in between the monitor cords and her trachea, noting that she was turning blue in the process, another nurse jumped over the overturned chairs and stretcher and pulled the cords from the wall. The patient bit, scratched and head butted me as I untangled the cords from around her neck. I grabbed my radio to scream for help, when she took advantage of one less hand on her and wrapped them around again!

As five nurses and EMT's wrestled her back onto the stretcher, placed her in 4-point leather restraints and gave her sedatives to calm her down, I sat on the floor, in the corner of the room, bruised and battered, wondering to myself, "What the hell am I doing? I am 48 years old and the main provider for three kids, if I get hurt what will we do?" I knew I had to get out. But how?

Soon after this event, a former manager had a proposition for me. She had a new position in her new clinic as an oncology nurse. I knew exactly nothing about oncology, but took a leap of faith, a Monday through Friday chemotherapy infusion job and doing psycho-social counseling for cancer patients. It was frightening, and I had a lot to learn. It wasn't perfect with a longer commute and less pay, but I did it anyway. I was making a difference in a new way and that decision, finally listening to that small voice within me, has put me on a path that has led me home to myself, the self I had forgotten ever existed.

There truly is a circle of life. The circle is the archetype for our lives. We begin (at conception… or do we?), and we end (at our last breath… or do we?) One thing leads into another which leads into another which widens our vision and our purpose. No matter how much we think we are stopping the merry-go-round or how much we want to get off, the circle continues. The earth rotates. The light turns to darkness and the darkness to light once again. Stir and repeat. The question I have is, am I simply riding or am I courageous enough to become the merry-go-round?

For me, the experience of this living and dying and rising again has come many times in my life. These "wake-up calls" have changed everything…in some cases the entire course of my life. As I reflect, truthfully, on them, they do not seem to be the big moments of life one would think they would be. Like the night I made the decision not to intubate my mother, which would have allowed her to breathe via machine, in the hopes her massive brain hemorrhage would somehow dissipate. Or the day my husband moved out of our family home which began the reality of what this concept of "divorce" would mean for me and my children. No. They came in subtle, quiet moments, in which looking back, were the exact moments that I not only made a decision, but KNEW that it was a decision based in truth and necessity. No more pretenses, no more illusions, or as my mother used to say, "No more ifs, ands, or buts!!"

The moment I knelt by a chair in my dining room with my hands on my husband's knee, begging for help and guidance in my utter confusion and isolation and his inability to respond or take care of me. The moment on the top of a hill, leaning against a tree, overlooking the edge of the grounds of my graduate school with someone I cared deeply for and the realization that what we both desperately wanted from each other was impossible for either of us to give. The moment I made a phone call to police from 2,500 miles away on the evening my dear friend confided she wanted to die.

These were moments that only lasted a few minutes each. However, they began a cascade that changed not only me, but those to whom I held most precious in my life. They held within them the decisions, the true knowing, which lead to the deaths of the parts of myself that no longer served me. This is what these moments foreshadowed. If I am honest, going through these times of sitting with the despair have led to some of the greatest moments of living my way into a more authentic life, which is true to myself and my gifts. I finally allowed myself to listen to myself.

I left California in May of 2016. I sold my beautiful, small, too expensive house and moved home again. I bought a little house a mile from downtown. I renovated it the way I wanted it to be. I made some hard choices throughout my life, and I have lived the consequences. Through this, I have circled back to where I belong. Is it perfect? No. Is it easy? No. Would I do it again? Absolutely.

How did listening to these wake-up calls change me? I now believe in miracles and that death truly leads to new life. Fear doesn't have the stranglehold on me, my thoughts, my intestines or my faith that it used to and that I allowed it to have on me. I learned that through the kindness, humility, compassion and vulnerability of others who are willing to walk these paths beside me, I can mine new ways of being strong. I learned that agenda, drama, and expectations of others are false constructs that lead to deeper unhappiness, disappointment and wasted adrenal hormones. I learned, slowly, to begin to live with what is and accept others as they are instead of trying to cajole, change or manipulate them into my way of thinking. And I learned that there really is nothing that I cannot live without... except maybe oxygen.

Maggie Perrone BSN, MA, OCN

Maggie Perrone is the Executive Director of Genuine Journeys, a company dedicated to creating and facilitating retreats and workshops that help participants experience and expand their spiritual lives. She has over 30 years' experience in Emergency and Oncology nursing, teaching and healing those in difficult emotional, spiritual and physical situations. Maggie is a dynamic speaker with a unique touch, skilled in speaking to that which inherently and individually resounds with and connects us all. Maggie has the rare ability to guide people in contemplating ethereal concepts and then bringing them down to the reality of everyday life. Her talks connect people to each other in our shared humanity. Thus, learning to come home to ourselves in the process. She holds a Masters of Arts Degree in Pastoral Ministry from St. John's Seminary in Camarillo, California.

www.genuinejourneys.com

maggie@genuinejourneys.com

"Yoga and meditation are my refuge."

—Kerry Timberlake

The Power of Intention

KERRY TIMBERLAKE, RN, BSN

I was washing dishes at a restaurant in the evenings while living in the mountains of Southern California. Unbelievably, in the midst of intense prayer, while asking for direction in a career path, the answer came to me like a command. A clear voice actually told me to be a nurse. This was stunning because prior to this, I had never heard voices or seen the unseen. I knew I had to listen and allow the path of my life to change drastically.

My first step was to become a Certified Nurses Aid. The first permanent hospital job I held was in a small country hospital that drew orthopedic patients. I was eventually assigned to the Emergency Department, so I studied to become a certified Emergency Medical Technician while I was waiting to be accepted into nursing school.

Death became an experience that was part of Emergency Room work. I encountered death by electrocution, fulminant pulmonary edema, cardiac arrest, and various types of trauma. It was confusing for me, how to process the feelings about death? A Humanities instructor mentioned a book by Raymond Moody called Life after Life. Moody shared his research of the Near-Death Experience, a journey of the soul after passing to the other side, then returning to complete one's life mission. There were profound underlying themes in this literature that could be applied in my own life and career as a nurse. The phenomena of unconditional love on the other side, the embrace of a fearlessness of death because life continues beyond death, the life review that causes a change in one's values of respecting others feelings, and a deep sense of interconnectedness in all beings. It was a life-changing read that gave me a different way to see reality. It was so revealing for me to understand that the souls whose lives we touch as health care workers can hear and see everything even when they seem to be unconscious or perhaps even passed. I would embrace this knowing into the next phase of my career. There were events that occurred making it clear to me that the power of intention is underestimated. Our intentions as health care workers that we bring to work reach far beyond what meets the eye.

After graduating from a community college with an Associates of Sciences degree in Nursing, I was fortunate to be selected for an extensive training program and mentorship in Coronary Care at the local hospital. The program was fantastic, and I enjoyed learning the details and the skills of critical care nursing. The CCU became my home for the next ten years and showed me just how powerful a role intention plays in healthcare.

I once had an elderly female patient who had been comatose for over a week. I would talk to her and send her words of encouragement. Her serum potassium levels were so dangerously unstable that she required potassium boluses steadily throughout the day, doses that would normally be lethal. At one point I was asked if I needed a break from her care because I must have appeared stressed. I knew in my heart that if I walked away from this assignment that she would not make it. One day while sitting at her bedside, her physician walked into the room, and she woke up from her coma. She took his hand and expressed how confused she was. She wondered why she lived through this difficult illness of hers? Her doctor turned around and said, "Because you have been in good hands." Wow! Isn't that the best kind of feeling that a job can give to someone?

One evening while trying to nap at home before going in for the night shift, it was apparent that something was not allowing me to rest deeply like I normally would have. As I walked into the back door of the Acute Coronary Care Unit, there was a strong sense of a presence. One of the nurses mentioned that I was going to need some roller skates for that night! Once inside the acute CCU, it was clear what had been reaching out to me. A very elderly woman was lying in one of the beds with two nurses at her side. They had been resuscitating her for hours. An overwhelming sense of compassion came over me as I was compelled to speak to her from across the room in a silent prayer. She needed to receive prayers of blessings and reassurance that it was okay to let go and to move on home to the Creator. My thoughts assured her that I would not keep her alive against her will. The nurses who had been working on her for hours noticed that she now had passed without any further complications. It was amazing to witness this meaningful example of the power of our intentions.

There was another patient who was comatose for days. She had progressed cancer and was recovering from surgery. It seemed as if she was lost in her coma, not able to come out. It was my assignment to work with her that day. I softly whispered to her, encouraging her to come to a decision about her situation. I whispered to her that she needed to make up her mind to get better and go forward with her life or to simply let go. I assured her that whatever decision she made it would be acceptable. She made up her mind soon afterward and chose to pass even though she was resuscitated later that day, her determination had overruled her hesitancy, and she was finally able to pass to the other side. I never discussed this with anyone, no one would understand me.

There was no support to validate these examples of the power of our words and intentions upon our patients at this time in our understanding. It became clear to me that the use of positive speech and expecting good outcomes was needed in the healing process and strongly influential in patient outcomes. It also became my passion to secretly be impacted over the years by watching how synchronicity presented itself. There were many instances where a physician would walk into his patient's room at essential moments. Life-threatening emergencies would occur just when the right staff was present to attend to the incident. I reached a high level of satisfaction to be part of a team that was able to effectively save lives, even against all the odds while working in the Coronary Care Unit.

I eventually decided to return to school for a BSN and choose a different nursing specialty. I was out of college for the summer working in an Intensive Care Unit when I met Jasmine. She was a beautiful 16-year-old who had been in a terrible automobile accident that year. She was very much loved by her family members. Her femur had been shattered causing fatty emboli that had been released and traveled distally in her body. She had lost most of her vision, some kidney function, fingertips, and toes. Her right leg had been amputated below the knee. She was so beautiful despite this misfortune. Her hair was very long and blond. Her eyes were a lovely light shade of blue. It was clear to me her eyes were filled with sadness and terror while she lived on the ventilator. She had been living in the ICU on life support systems for the last six months. I felt so helpless while attending to her medical needs. It was a painful feeling, wanting to do so much more for her. There was nothing more anyone could do.

While approaching my senior year in a Baccalaureate program for Nursing at a progressive university, it was time to pick a senior clinical project for completion of the degree. As an RN for the last ten years, I had wanted to learn something new. It was an important decision, knowing that this was a path that could impact my future. I considered specializing in biofeedback, but that would require having equipment in order to function. Jin Shin Jyutsu caught my attention, an ancient healing art that moves energy through the body by touching a combination of points on the body. This seemed like a skill that I could take anywhere. I was blessed to have an opportunity to take my first five-day seminar on Jin Shin Jyutsu with Mary Burmeister, the woman who founded this healing modality in America in the 1950's after her studies in Japan. Jin Shin Jyutsu incorporates the use of positive intention. It is translated as the creator's art through compassionate man. The whole point of Jin Shin Jyutsu is to offer encouragement for self-healing. Ultimately healing happens when the logical mind gets out of the way, and self-healing is allowed. Our cells are constantly regenerating and renewing themselves and doing an excellent job maintaining a state of health and balance.

During my studies, I had to choose a number of clients that would commit to having a free one hour long Jin Shin Treatment twice weekly for a period of three months. There was an office on campus to do treatments in, plus I also found people that would come to my home. The assignment was to keep a record of vital signs before and after treatments plus a log of any progress towards any symptom relief. That is when I remembered Jasmine. I eventually reached her Mom by phone one day after weeding through the phone book and trying to find the right home. Her mother said, "Well, we don't have anything to lose." She agreed to let her daughter try Jin Shin Jyutsu. Jasmine had been bedridden, never going anywhere except to doctor appointments and dialysis for the last two months. Her life was to change yet again.

She came to my private residence for Jin Shin Jyutsu treatments for three months. She initially got around in a wheelchair, then dragged herself onto a cot set up for her to recline on in my living room. The treatments gave Jasmine a reason to get out of bed and to participate in life again. I focused on improvements in her circulation, vision, kidney functions, and whatever the pulses had directed me to do that day. Jasmine progressed from the wheelchair to being fitted with a prosthesis over her leg and walking with a walker. She smiled and was acting more like her old self. It wasn't long before she was using crutches to get around. In the last weeks of her treatments, she was even progressing socially and could walk without the crutches. She was planning on going back to school and she felt ready for college. She wanted an apartment of her own. I was very pleased to see her go through such tremendous changes.

I never knew what happened to her after her treatments were finished, but feel thankful to have known her. She was a stimulus for me to choose a nursing specialty such as energy work that could be done wherever my path led me as an RN.

I wanted to use more Jin Shin Jyutsu in my work at the hospital, after all, it is a skill that is based on compassion, plus had no unwanted effects. Energy medicine is a means to reach the soul level of healing. I encountered resistance from the manager who felt it would be necessary to have permission from a patient's primary care physician before using Jin Shin. I knew that would hold me back from using Jin Shin so I decided that I'd stay in the flow of the moment and would seek permission from a patient if it seemed like a little Jin Shin would be helpful.

While working in a Labor and Delivery department one day, there was a woman who had been in labor for the last four hours without cervical dilation beyond six centimeters. It was clear that per standards of practice, she was an overdue candidate for a Cesarean Section. She was surrounded by a large number of family members who wanted to be there to witness this birth. They were all talking with seemingly little regard for what the mother was feeling. Uncomfortably, I pushed myself to be forceful and requested that the family let her have just a little time alone. After they had left her room, I attempted to make sure that she was as comfortable as she could be under the circumstances. Her permission was requested to try some energy work to see if this might be helpful. After consenting, she was encouraged to relax and focus on her breathing while I worked on moving the blocked energy. I spent perhaps ten minutes with her, then I was needed to attend at an imminent delivery, so I left, but later happily learned that she did have a normal vaginal birth of a healthy baby girl. I am certain that the relaxation and the Jin Shin Jyutsu had played a beneficial role in her labor progressing to a normal delivery.

In my core, I can feel a deep sense of value as a nurse who brings both positive intentions and skills to transform situations at work into outcomes that benefit my patients. Nursing is a fabulous means to be present during some of the most important moments of a person's life. This makes for innumerable instances that healing occurs by the power of positive intentions backed by the respected skills of a registered nurse. I often feel tremendously grateful that I was directed to be a nurse and wonder about the source that guided me to this path. It was certainly a divine inspiration that has taken me on a sustainable and gratifying journey.

Kerry Timberlake, RN, BSN

Kerry Timberlake began practicing Hatha Yoga at the age of 16. The next year, 1968, she met with the Maharishi Mahesh Yogi to become initiated into the practice of Transcendental Meditation. In those days, meditation lasted for an hour a day. As an adult, she explored different religions and sought out different styles of meditation practice. Kerry worked and supported herself through nursing school. She spent a lot of time hiking in nature, abalone and scuba diving in the ocean, or gardening, and eventually married a European who wanted to travel the world. They took their backpacks and continuously traveled the world for nearly a year. Kerry later explored different healing techniques such as toning, shamanic healing, dream work, hypnotism, and healing with colors. She organized a community discussion group for the Institute of Noetic Sciences for five years to explore spirituality and science. In the process of returning to college for a BSN, Kerry began doing energy work called Jin Shin Jyutsu, traveling to join Native American spiritual gatherings in different states over the US to absorb native wisdoms. She especially enjoys exploring intuition or inner ways of knowing. She has worked in nursing for 44 years and continues to work full time as an RN.

https://www.facebook.com/kerry.timberlake

kertim@earthlink.net

"Life isn't about waiting for the storm to pass...

It's about learning to dance in the rain."

—Vivian Greene

Angels, Heartbeats, and Stethoscopes

CAROLINE J. WHEELER RN, BSN

Bill shouted, stormed past me, grabbed the .44 Magnum from the table, flung open the door, and stomped out, slamming it behind him. We waited for the bang.

Minutes seemed liked hours, with an instant rush of fear and adrenalin, I studied the walk-in closet to my right and thought if he returns with the gun, I'll dive into it as I've seen in the movies.

We were visiting a hospice patient in an unstable, unsafe home, and needed to leave immediately. Earlier that morning I'd learned there was a son who lived nearby, who'd be shot by his father if he ever set foot on this property. Ushering Jill, towards the door, we left through the kitchen, past the cleaning lady, silent, wide-eyed and pale, clutching her broom. We stepped out the front door. Suddenly, Jill yelled, "Run, it's the f**king son!" (I had never heard Jill curse, ever! This was serious!)

Sprinting to the car, I yanked open the passenger door and jumped in. I looked over my shoulder and saw my colleague backed up against the trunk of the car. With his finger pointing right in her face, the son was yelling, accusing her of cutting off his Dad's meds and hospice service. I couldn't leave her out there, so I stepped out of the car, and she yelled, "Call the office." I retreated inside the car, called our office, and gave a hurried report to our RN supervisor, who said she would call 911.

We heard a shout from the house, "Leave those girls alone!" Bill ordered his son, who calmed slightly and took a few steps back from Jill. Safely inside the car, we closed the doors, gratefully driving away.

I called 911 to report we were okay. However, they tell me that once they initiate a call; the dispatcher cannot cancel it. No more than a quarter mile down the road we saw an ambulance, lights flashing and sirens screaming towards us, followed by a Sheriff's car, and another, and a black SUV with lights flashing. We felt helpless. The 911 dispatcher told me we should park at the side of the road and wait to be debriefed by the sheriff.

This was my second week in my new hospice job. New to the town, however not new to hospice, this day would remain the most frightening of all my 25 years as a nurse.

Many emotions, reflection on my hospice career and thoughts of improving safety went through my mind. Safety is a priority for health professionals who perform home visits. Dogs, weapons, drugs, alcohol intoxication, inclement weather, severe driving conditions, and even family conflicts can pose potential hazards.

Hospice is incredibly valuable, still unknown to many people, yet those who use this service express their gratitude and relief during every visit. I have been asked many times, "Isn't it a depressing job?" I reply that hospice allows the person to live the rest of their days with dignity in the comfort of their own home with family, pets and familiar surroundings. They maintain control and a quality of life with their loved ones, receiving support, education, equipment, professional nursing care including instruction on medication and symptom management. Patients have access to the entire hospice team, a holistic approach to care many families report they could not have done without.

Hospice is worldwide and far from a new concept. As far back as 11th Century Europe, weary or ill travelers were given food, shelter, and care in 'hospices.' In 1879, Our Lady's Hospice, in Dublin, Ireland opened its doors. England's Dame Cicely Saunders initiated care for the terminally ill, in 1948, opening St Christopher's Hospice in 1967. It was here she died, in 2005. The first hospice home visit and first hospice house in the United States were seen in 1974, in Connecticut.

A hospice nurse wears many hats and looks through many lenses. Some people call us angels. Clinical knowledge, experience, and a myriad of skills are combined with the ability to establish rapport, communicate effectively in all kinds situations, and be with people in the manner they need. You are a guest in your patient's home, during one of the most profound, stressful, and emotionally difficult times of their lives. Gaining their trust is paramount. Compassion, empathy, and acceptance merge with critical thinking, planning, and innovation. You combine your head and your heart as a nurse in the hospice world.

Five years ago, my dad told me of his prostate cancer diagnosis over the phone. I flew home to New Zealand to visit him and to say goodbye. I stayed with him and his partner, whom I'd never met, in a home I'd never seen, in a town I'd never visited. Observing physical limitations, the walker, the decline and fatigue are much harder when it's your own loved one. Dad had fallen several days prior, requiring surgery on his hand and IV antibiotics, so a District Nurse was visiting him regularly. It was strangely comforting, yet, ironic witnessing a home visit by an RN, who performed the same tasks as I usually did, 7,500 miles away in Oregon, USA.

During one of the days there, I walked down to the mall and found a woman selling Maori pendants. We talked about my visit, and how she had cared for her father in similar circumstances. I bought several pendants for my friends back home, and a couple for myself. One was a beautiful large ornate fish hook, with New Zealand Paua shell set in metal, symbolizing health and prosperity. It was wrapped carefully with the others and stowed in my bag.

On my last day with Dad, my aunt and uncle arrived, and we all had lunch. The five of us talked, took photos, and said our goodbyes. I hugged Dad, knowing this would be the last time I'd see him, yet not quite believing it. I went back for a second hug, then watched out the back window as he waved while we drove away. I choked back the tears.

Back in Oregon, I continued visiting patients in their homes, assisted living facilities, and adult foster homes. In hospice 'home' is defined as wherever the patient is living, as long as it's not designated skilled care, like in a nursing home. With a deeper understanding of the struggle, anticipatory grief, and the bargaining, people experience as death approaches, I reflected on how we're taught to keep our boundaries. We're expected to care as we provide care, yet keep a distance.

However, nursing is a science and an art. Understanding, being present and human with your patient and their family is required, in addition to the clinical aspects. True empathy is developed and can be authentically demonstrated when our own experiences have been so close to those of who we're with. The months prior to visiting my father, and my visit I had with him added another layer of empathy for me personally and as a hospice nurse. Although no one's experience is the same, to say I understand that genuine empathy was a comfort I was now able to provide.

Anytime, though commonly after midnight, an on-call hospice nurse will attend a patient death. The nurse pronounces death, though not every country requires this. This assessment can be one of the most heart-wrenching, with everyone's eyes on you, or you may be tucked away, out of sight, with the recently deceased loved one. The stethoscope is one of the most common clinical tools of the hospice nurse trade. Used every home visit for vital signs, checking heart rate, lung sounds, and bowel sounds. Patients, their families, and caregivers take great comfort in seeing this clinical assessment performed.

Providing compassion, bringing comfort to someone, sometimes a stranger, during or after the death of a loved one is a significant aspect of hospice nursing, making it such a meaningful profession. One Sunday afternoon I was able to provide this compassion and empathy to a mother and daughter. My stethoscope became the grim tool of confirmation of death for a daughter who couldn't believe her father had just died before our eyes. In disbelief, she asked, "Please, listen one more time." I did, and then pleading, "I can't believe he's gone, he looks the same, please listen one more time..." The stethoscope becomes so significant, taking on its most impactful role as we listen for one minute for the heart rate or its absence, before pronouncing death.

A few months later, my sister called me from Dad's bedside, as he lay unresponsive. I pictured a hospice nurse in his room, listening to his lungs. My sister held her phone to Dad's ear, I could hear his slow, deep breaths, I spoke to him, told him I loved him, and what a great Dad he had been. It is widely known that in an unresponsive state, a person can still hear, this and pain sensation are the final senses to leave. The next day my father died, peacefully, and comfortably, his lady sleeping in a nearby chair, in the hospice house, with care provided by nurses, working in the same role as me, across the Pacific Ocean.

One of my patients, I saw in his own home, for just a short time. He had ALS, a neurological disease resulting in progressive weakness, loss of motor function, difficulty swallowing and breathing, though the mind remains sharp. Knowing what lay ahead, he had decided to take advantage of Oregon's Death with Dignity Act and was planning for this in a few days. Hospice neither prolongs, nor hastens death, and most hospice services do not permit their staff to be present during this event. We can, however, support the family afterward.

When I met my patient's daughter, and she learned I was from New Zealand; she was intrigued. She revealed she had worked closely with a Maori healer, who travels the world. I told her though it was just a fraction, 1/64, I was part Maori myself.

The day arrived, three of my patient's friends had been invited to be present when he legally ended his life. I was asked to visit beforehand, and they knew I couldn't be present when he took the medication. Before I left home that morning, I saw the Maori fish hook pendant and placed it in my pocket, thinking if it seemed appropriate, I would give this to the daughter.

I walked up the stone steps to their home and was let in by my patient's wife. I greeted his daughter; she gave me a hug. I brought out the pendant, saying, "I bought this in New Zealand while I was visiting my father who was dying. I'd like you to have it." I explained what it symbolized. She accepted it gladly with tears streaming down her face, then she rushed out of the room, and up the stairs. Her mother said gratefully that those were the first tears her daughter had shed since arriving. At the time I bought the pendant, I had no idea it would bring such meaning to a person I hadn't even met, halfway across the world. This was one of my most memorable and meaningful, hospice moments.

We are encouraged not to have favorites; however, I did have a favorite hospice patient. I'd visit two to three times a week, bringing her medication, setting up the weekly medminder, and visiting with a cup of tea after her vital signs were taken and discussed.

This patient and her husband were simply a joy to visit. They both maintained such a positive attitude, never complained, and I was presented with the best cup of tea in my very own mug on every visit! My patient confided she'd always get up out of bed in the morning, no matter how difficult or how long it took. Her husband helped her to dress; she'd put on some makeup, and with determination make the journey to the living room chair where she could sit and look out at their yard filled with flowers. Too debilitated to do any more gardening herself, she accepts this decline and enjoys the yard through the window.

The determination in this lady was admirable. One or two times a day she would walk slowly without her walker, (despite my cautionary tales of patient falls), from her chair to the kitchen and back, resting halfway on a strategically placed stool. No longer able to cook, it was now her daily goal to make it to the kitchen and back, once or twice a day.

One day I was given a bag of small crystal angels, made by another patient, for us to give to our patients. I made my rounds over the next few days, having patients select which little angel they would like. Each patient took one with a smile. I arrived at my favorite patient's home and offered her a choice of two crystal angels. She happily chose the purple-tinted one, and her husband hung it on her walker, which although was never used, was always right beside her chair. Now the angel was suspended from her walker so she could see it every day.

Years later, I still have my crystal angel hanging in my car, a gentle reminder of how precious life is, and though we may become fragile, our determination and spirit can remain strong. Not everyone believes in angels. However, for some patients and their families, hospice nurses, (and the whole team, including office staff), are angels. Angels who answer phone calls, bring supplies for comfort, providing skilled care, compassion, instruction, and reassurance right to the end. Often to the very last breath, their loved one takes on this earth. Then the angel takes the stethoscope and listens for the heartbeat…

Caroline J. Wheeler RN, BSN

Caroline J. Wheeler was born in Christchurch, New Zealand. She graduated in 1992 with a Bachelor of Health Science (Nursing) and worked in Wellington, in community and inpatient mental health. She then moved to the United States, passed the NCLEX (board exam), and continued her nursing career.

Caroline's experience encompasses 25 years, predominantly home health and hospice, mental health, med/surgical, and long-term care/ memory care. Whenever she leaves a job the most common statements of farewell are, "We'll miss your smile," and, "You're a breath of fresh air."

A Hospice Medical Director once asked her to be the nurse for his father. As Director of a large Oregon Hospice, he had many nurses to choose from. This remains one of the highlights of her career.

Living on the Oregon Coast, Caroline loves photography, kayaking, the outdoors, seafood, and beach walks. She loves to travel, whether it's road trips, exploring the United States, or the World. She loves meeting people, socializing, and helping others. She loves cats and always has one or two rescue kitties. Owner/ member of Wheeler Marketing Group, LLC, a healthcare copywriting/ content marketing business, Caroline also works part-time in a clinical role, to maintain her contact with patients.

www.WheelerMarketingGroup.com

carolinejwheeler@gmail.com

"My religion is very simple. My religion is kindness."

—Dalai Lama

Mother Earth Speaks

CATHERINE MEDICINE HEART R.N., CHT, PNP, M.DIV.

It is 1967; I am dressed from head to toe in white. Sensible and sturdy white shoes, white support hose, crisply ironed white uniform and the ephemeral starched white nurse cap, perched upon my 1960s-bouffant hairdo. It is the very first day of nursing school clinic at the local General Hospital, in my hometown. Our nursing instructor, a retired Army nurse (seriously), is leading our small group of student nurse newbies down the hall to our very first assignment.

As we enter the room, we see a woman lying still on a gurney hooked up to an IV. We notice the skin on her entire upper body appears to be covered in exposed fat eruptions. It does not take very long for us astonished first-day nursing students to realize the woman is deceased. Amid my own unsuspecting shock and disbelief, at seeing my first deceased person, our nursing instructor directs us to disconnect the IV and prepare this deceased person to be placed into a black body bag, and we dutifully proceed.

The only thing our instructor says is, "This is what happens when you stick your head into a gas oven." We leave the room with our task completed, and I realize a major eye-opening event has just occurred, and that my coping mechanism, is to tuck this shocking experience away into a mental compartment labeled, "Well, here you go into the field of nursing!" As I reflect upon this early experience in my nursing career, I realize that it was perhaps a catalyzing event that influenced my path to follow the calling of natural health and plant healing medicine.

From nursing school training, my first work experience was at the local psychiatric state hospital. I smile at the thought of myself as a 21-year-old new nursing graduate, stepping into locked Ward A26. "A" standing for ACUTE psychiatric, and #26, "Ward number." It was here on Ward A26, that I once again had my internal psyche assaulted and eyes opened, regarding my new profession. This time to the unknown world of the "mentally ill."

My very first week on this ward I remember a young woman close to my own age, who after having an outburst, was manhandled by two male orderlies, pinned down, and as one of the RNs on duty, I was required to inject a very large shot of Thorazine into her left buttocks! Naturally, though unknown to me at the time, my codependent nurse self, had all my attention focused on being a "good responsible nurse," performing the expected duties of my position and job description.

Today I realize that under the surface, I had been horrified by this overt and overwhelming violence to another human. In my few months on that acute psychiatric ward, I later befriended that same young woman. As I learned more about who she was, it seemed to me; she had just the same basic unmet needs of understanding, which any young person has, without owning coping mechanisms skills or having human emotional support.

After only nine months at the psychiatric hospital, Ronald Reagan our new California State governor decided to close all the California state hospitals. I was transferred to the San Francisco Bay Area, to work at a mental health center at the University of California. I only lasted three months at this big city hospital, as it was too high paced for my country girl upbringing. Once again, the trauma of watching depressed young women being rolled away on gurneys for electroshock treatment and returning in an incoherent state was affecting my sensibilities regarding medical, psychiatric practices.

Driving across the Golden Gate Bridge and taking up residency in a small Marin County town, was my turning point into the world of natural health and natural medicine. Here in the early 1970's, vegetarianism, natural health remedies and homebirth was the prevailing lifestyle for all of us young burgeoning "hippies" of the peace and love generation.

Probably the most impactful beginning event of my connection to earth medicine was finding myself at age 23, with a one-year old-child, and the need to escape a very abusive and broken relationship. A friend found me a temporary home in the mountains between Napa and Sonoma, living in a tipi! Here I would hike a quarter-mile, with my young son on my back, to gather fresh spring water for drinking. Another friend showed me how to identify and harvest wild soap root plant, with which I used to scrub and hand wash my clothes. I also received the gift of learning to identify wild herbs for eating and making tea.

At age 25, eight months pregnant with my second child and traveling to find a country home in northern Oregon, I experienced my first personal homebirth delivery. I was delighted during this time, to also find my first book on natural herbal healing by Jethro Gloss and I began practicing those remedies with my family. Little did I know, after the birth of my second child at home, that I would have a destined homebirth midwifery calling. A month after my first daughter was born, a young neighbor asked me to assist in the delivery of her first child. I quickly became the local midwife, needing to learn how to be a skilled homebirth practitioner.

During this time of learning to become a homebirth practitioner, I experienced another event that was to become a pivotal moment in how natural healing medicine became a way of life for me. A friend from my hometown in California invited myself and my two younger sisters to assist him and his wife in the natural homebirth of their first child. After a wonderful birthing experience, and getting everyone settled in, the new father encouraged me to go out into the yard to find prolifically growing flowers call Calendula. The new father said this flower was extremely valuable for healing the skin.

Opening the garden gate and walking into the garden I was greeted by abundantly low growing single petaled orange and golden yellow flowers. My closer examination revealed large clusters of seed pods on each flowering plant, as abundant as the flowers themselves. Without a second thought, I began gathering fistfuls of seeds, my first in a lifetime of harvesting Calendula flowers and seeds.

After my research on how to use Calendula flowers, I began planting the crescent-shaped seeds everywhere, then harvesting the flowers and making a beautiful golden tincture from their petals. The result, as I began experimenting with using this tincture for my new moms birthing wounds (lacerations, tears, skid marks, etc.) was that I had in my hands, the most magnificent and miraculous healing substance. It visually astounded me, time after time, with its speed for healing. As I continued to explore natural alternative healing tools for my midwife bag, I began to realize, from a very deep inner place, what a gift it was. Soon my homebirth delivery bag was filled with hand-harvested herbs for pregnancy, homemade tinctures for delivery and postpartum care, and other assorted herbal remedies for mom and baby.

As the years passed, I increased my experience and knowledge regarding homebirth practices and the use of natural medicine. In the very beginning of this life phase, I noticed a pattern. At each homebirth I attended, I would receive a teaching that was intrinsically the next step of knowledge needed for this practice. Was there some divine hand choreographing this unfolding journey of service? It makes so much sense now that the experience of tracking where a woman was in her labor progression, the great need to be constantly observing and sensing a laboring woman's needs was a most fertile ground for developing a greater understanding and communion with the subtle energies that are always present.

I remember at one birth, the birthing women seemed to be struggling with some internal challenge, and was not progressing well with her cervical dilation at a steady rate. My midwife assistant and I were discussing and wondering what the possible blockage could be. At that moment, I felt a part of myself connecting into the mother and child. I clearly sensed that the baby in her womb communicated to me a question to ask the mom. I asked the question, and the mom acknowledged that it was indeed the powerful emotional challenge she was facing.

The holy humble Calendula flower continued to bring me amazing gifts to support my practice of midwifery and natural healing wisdom. In the early 1980s, after giving birth to my third child (second homebirth), I was privileged to live during the summer season, on a beautiful mountaintop farm in the Hood River Valley with a most magnificent view of Mount Hood.

Upon moving to the farm, I of course, immediately planted Calendula seeds, and as the Calendula flowers began to flower prolifically, a friend suggested I send fresh flowers to a homeopathic company back east. I was surprised at her suggestion, as I had heard of homeopathy but did not realize that Calendula flowers were part of that healing modality. Subsequently, I sent fresh Calendula flowers to the company, they welcomed my harvest, and returned to me, in trade, some basic homeopathic remedies for family first aid, as well as remedies to use in my midwifery practice. Thus began, a whole new area of research and discovery, adding more amazing tools for family healing, labor and delivery support, and once again, activating my constant amazement at the power of nature, and the historical use of natural healing in our world.

As I began to trust the power of intuition, even more, I could feel how wisdom expands through observing and listening. I glimpsed the many levels of conscious awareness available beyond the "normal 3-D world." I was especially in awe of observing the subtle power of homeopathic remedies, and came to rely on those "little white pills," and herbal tinctures, who felt like dear friends who would always show up when needed. Intuiting communications from the plant kingdom world, also became a way of life, as my love for wildcrafting plants to make my own medicines, was the most thrilling pastime and continues to be to this day.

There is a code among herbalists, that when harvesting plants in the wild, you only ever take one-third or less of each species in an area, as an honoring to the entire plant kingdom. As I religiously practiced this code of ethics to wildcrafting, I began to notice and realize that the plants of a particular species that I was harvesting, would literally direct me to where I could find more abundance of that same plant. This delighted me beyond words and filled me with such sublime gratitude for this world of immensely unseen interspecies communication.

These decades of teaching and practicing natural health are a deep reminder of my lifelong passion for honoring plant wisdom healing and to the phenomenal experiences of supporting the homebirth movement. In honoring my own deep commitment and dedication to supporting life, and appreciating the natural world, I understand clearly the impact of my early nursing career that influenced my chosen path. I walk with deep gratitude for my life, dedicated to this path of natural healing and human birthing support. It has and continues to be, an opportunity to experience life with a richness that feels divinely inspired and surpasses my greatest imaginations and dreams.

Our Mother Earth speaks, and I shall always listen.

Catherine Medicine Heart R.N., CHT, PNP, M.Div.

Catherine Medicine Heart has been a natural health practitioner and educator, in numerous fields of complementary and alternative medicine, for the past 45 years. For 25 of those years, she provided homebirth midwifery support to scores of women, wanting to have alternative birthing experiences.

Her many fields of alternative medicine education and practice have included: herbal medicine, nutrition & healthy lifestyle, homeopathy, clinical transpersonal hypnotherapy, neurofeedback & biofeedback, traumatic birth release therapy, and Native American healing practices.

In 2007, she received a Masters of Divinity degree, becoming an ordained Minister of Peace, through the Beloved Community of Spiritual Peacemaking.

Presently, as a grandmother to three grandsons, and a part-time functional medicine nurse, she enjoys educating others about the use of pure essential oils for health and well-being, and provides natural health consulting.

Ms. Heart resides in the Santa Cruz Mountains of the Central California Coast, where she spends every spare moment being in the natural world of wild plants, animals, and majestic Redwood trees.

https://www.facebook.com/ arthearthealingessentials/

medicineheart@gmail.com

"We have to continue to learn. We have to be open. And we have to be ready to release our knowledge in order to come to a higher understanding of reality."

—Thich Nhat Hanh

Seeds of Awareness

MELINDA JAHN, RN

I actually went to nursing school twice. Granted the first time was for only four days before I dropped out, but still, I think it's relevant to my story. The first time I went into the nursing program, I just couldn't do it. It felt very rigid, judgemental, rule oriented, and somewhat threatening. It wasn't a place where I felt like I could thrive. I felt like nursing school might not be conducive to my mental health, or support my personal philosophies in life. I'm an interesting mix of a person. I'm wild and rebellious, but also sensitive and intuitive. Because of my wild, boisterous side, my sensitive intuitiveness is often overlooked, and not noticed.

After I dropped out of nursing school, I couldn't let it go. It didn't feel right that I quit. I had worked hard to earn my spot. I didn't care if I ever worked as a nurse, but I needed to prove to myself that I could finish the program, so I went back.

I've done a lot of personal work in my life. It is my goal to evolve into the highest version of myself. I'm not always very graceful or eloquent or soft-spoken. I've fallen a lot, but have an innate resiliency that has served me well. Years before I ever went to nursing school, I had a therapist who introduced me to the writings of Thich Nhat Hanh, and that is where I believe I became aware of my journey into mindfulness and energy. I remember a part of his book, Anger, where Hanh wrote about chickens and eggs, and if the hen was distressed and we ate her egg, we would take in that distressed energy--or something along those lines. That story still resonates with me today, because we are energy-sensitive creatures, and I believe that is the root of much physical and mental illness we suffer from today. It is under that premise that I began to study energy medicine and how to integrate this awareness into the nursing world.

Two years after I dropped out of nursing school, there I sat again, in the classroom, grateful that I got into the nursing program for a second time, when my professor started reading different nursing diagnoses to the class. She read out loud while scoffing, "Disturbed Energy Field," then proceeded to talk about how stupid and nonsensical it was, and went off on a tangent about evidence-based practice, and I just sat there thinking to myself, "But that is the most important nursing diagnosis I've heard!" So again, I didn't really feel like I fit in the class, but I was resolved to reach my goal and finish nursing school.

During my first year of training, one patient's story, in particular, holds a place in my memory. She was a sweet lady in her mid-sixties who was in the hospital because she needed a skin graft. You see, she had sleep-walked outside in the freezing cold while on Ambien and slipped and fell and couldn't get up. She had frostbite and subsequently needed the skin graft.

I asked her how long she had had trouble sleeping, and she confided in me that she hadn't slept well since she was a young girl. She had alcoholic parents who would fight violently and throw things. When her parents passed out, she'd get up in the night to clean up their mess. This is another example of the distressed chicken and the egg.

My patient took in her parents' unhealthy energy, internalized it as her own, and eventually, it manifested as physical illness. I can see this pattern time and time again, but because it isn't based on scientific evidence, it doesn't fall under proper nursing guidelines. We could diagnose this as "Disturbed Energy Field," but that nursing diagnosis has been challenged, and is literally scoffed at by much of the nursing profession.

Time went on, and I graduated nursing school. Woo Hoo! I did it! I accomplished my goal and accepted my first nursing position in a Cardiology clinic. Even though our patients were treated pharmaceutically, I saw so much missed opportunity in the treatment of our patients. If it wasn't a statin, it didn't appear to hold too much priority or merit in our clinic. The providers I worked for were very logical, linear thinkers, and had no apparent room for thinking alternatively. While I respected their knowledge and intellects, I felt sorry for them for missing such a critical role in healthcare. It was ironic to me that these people worked to treat people's cardiac disorders, yet seemed so absolutely out of touch with the obvious metaphors of the heart. They could see the energy on an EKG but were blind to the healing energy that we could provide in other ways. It disappointed me, and needless to say, I moved on after only six months.

I asked myself what I could do as a nurse when I saw these patterns, yet was obligated to practice nursing under strict guidelines and regulations, and to be honest, I am still trying to answer that question.

I now work as a behavioral health nurse with the persistently and severely mentally ill population. One would deduce that if any patient were ever to have a disturbed energy field, it would be a mentally ill person, but even psychiatrists, like cardiologists, are pharmaceutically driven. I'd love to implement an energy group, but lack hope of that happening under our current medical system.

I began studying energy medicine last year, and continue to grow my awareness and knowledge. We can all feel energy. When someone walks into a room, we can feel the energy either positive, negative or somewhere in between. This is particularly important for nurses. If a nurse doesn't do the necessary personal work to get his/her energy balanced, it will be impossible to help with a patient's energy. This is where I believe compassion fatigue comes from.

There are many ways to get balanced energy—just a few include breathing and meditation, yoga, meridian work, being in nature, and grounding exercises. If we as nurses don't take time for personal wellness and reflection, it won't be possible for us to help our patients. We too often hear of nurses who work 12-hour shifts without even using the restroom. This is inappropriate and unacceptable and needs to shift. We as nurses need to prioritize self-care in order to care for our patients adequately. By loving ourselves, we can love our patients, which is the ultimate healing energetic force.

This also brings up the idea of how nurses "eat their young." Where on earth was that mentality born? How does that build on positive healing energy? I for one will never subscribe to that idea and believe that it is nonsensical at best and dangerous at worst. Who wants to go to work to serve others only to be let loose in a lion's den? How can we do our best work and reach our highest potential in an environment that is not supportive and uplifting?

It goes without saying that as nurses, our technical skills and critical thinking need to be second to none, but what is missing to some extent is this energetic work of which this book is about. It isn't complicated at all. When we are sick, all we really want is to be loved and taken care of. It is no fun not to feel well, and it is frightening to be vulnerable. By simply bringing good, loving energy and presence to our patients, we can begin the healing cascade. Whether it is a warm wet washcloth on an old man's face, or more advanced energy techniques such as tracing meridians, clearing chakras or moving energy with crystals and magnets, the first step is awareness. Because we cannot change things, we are not aware of.

It is my hope that as the field of medicine evolves from a symptom-based model to a preventative based one, we can find creative ways to help teach our patients to help themselves. A critical role in wellness is energy. People can learn to tune into their own energy and feel things in their own energy fields before they manifest physically.

I think it would be amazing to see school-based clinics teach energy work to young pupils. For kids to learn to separate their energy from others would be incredible--not only for at-risk, disadvantaged kids but for all children. Energy work could be especially helpful for children who have endured sexual, emotional or physical abuse. Teaching kids to tune into how they truly feel energetically could greatly reduce physical and mental diseases later down the road. Teaching kids to cope through energy holds great potential.

Our senior population is also beginning to wake up energetically. Increased awareness can shift behavior, and change health--even chronic health problems. If in our nursing assessments, we performed some simple energy tests, we could plant seeds of awareness and empower our patients with tools that encourage true healing--not just treating symptoms with medications.

It is my hope that the future of holistic nursing will embrace and encourage energy medicine as part of an integrated model of healing. There is so much potential to help people in ways that we are just beginning to scratch the surface of. I am thankful for the opportunity to contribute to this compilation of voices in this book and proud to have a small part in what I can see as becoming a revolution in healthcare.

Melinda Jahn, RN

Melinda Jahn is a free spirit who wants the most out of life. She is an optimist who believes in the good in the world and wants to spread her idealism to places far and wide. Melinda loves her family, her dogs, her chickens, and sometimes even her evil cat, Trixie. In her free time, Melinda can be found hiking, cooking, paddle boarding, acting in community theater, practicing yoga, driving her kids around, or reading a good book (she still likes paper). She has also been spotted at happy hour from time to time. Her professional endeavors include nursing, real estate, and Medicare insurance in no particular order. She has been married for nearly 19 years to a Danish man named Henrik. She is grateful for all the abundance in her life and believes in the power of light and laughter.

Aboutbend.com

"You have to master not only the art of listening to your head, you must also master listening to your heart and listening to your gut."

—Carly Fiorina

Found A Way

SHARON BULLER, BSN, RN

I was drawn into nursing after working in the school system for a few years in the special needs classroom. I decided to go back to school and what I really wanted was to be a veterinarian. Silly me, I thought that I was not smart enough, so I went into nursing. The joke was on me with my first hospital clinical. I was so upset realizing that I was not able to truly make a difference the way I truly wanted to. I had no control. As I chased a doctor down to make sure that my patient was covered for the pain that was keeping him from moving forward in his healing, I realized what a huge mistake I had made. I was too far into the education and too deep in the money I owed to stop my nursing path. I knew I had to find a way to make it work.

After graduation and being informed that I would not be allowed to go on into a Nurse Practitioner Program, I had been told I must work in a hospital for a year prior to entering. I knew once I was working and no longer living in poverty that I would not return. I went to work in a hospital where my patients were newborn to centenarian, along with post-op to hospice care there. The patient load was frightening and dangerous with seven patients to one nurse. If I was very lucky, I would get a CNA to work with. The nurses that were working there before me treated me with great disrespect, to the point of setting me up for mistakes that thankfully I discovered prior to anything happening to any of my patients. That lasted a little more than nine months when I found another position in another hospital. I moved into a medical detox program working alongside a great doctor, using some great tools including acupuncture to assist in the detox. Unfortunately, that program was closed after about a year due to being unprofitable for the hospital.

I then joined an RN staffing company and went all over the valley working in private homes, doctor's offices and hospitals. For a few years, this was a very interesting education. Since you could pick and choose what jobs you wanted to do, I added in public health at that point getting a part-time job to go along with the agency. I had enjoyed my public health experience while in school, as I felt like I was able to work directly with the client and make more of an impact in their life than inpatient care in an office or hospital. I moved into a full-time temporary position working a Hepatitis A outbreak in another county. That lasted about a year. After that, another county another public health position, this one included a high-risk mother and baby, the county jail, a refugee program, STD clinician, and HIV case manager. After awhile I could not handle the stress and running into clients on the street, so I left.

I started my own business at that point as a consulting RN. I began with a couple of Special Needs group homes and expanded to working with a few attorneys reviewing medical records for them. I spent eight years as the consulting RN in a group of brain-injured homes. During this time, I also worked as an Adjunct Professor for about three years in a community nursing clinical position. Once the "health care" was taken over by the government all my contracts were swallowed up, and my hourly pay dropped $20.00 immediately. I became overwhelmed by all the paperwork and getting anything for my clients became a constant battle.

When I was attending nursing school, I was introduced to Healing Touch, reading auras, and using the breath by an amazing RN. That stayed with me from that day forward in every cell of my body. I truly believe it was my opening to trusting my intuition.

Through the years I studied other energy healing modalities that I know have saved my life and made a difference for others. I came to feel that Allopathic medicine can put the body back together, but the healing can only happen in the body with its healing energy.

My first big Aha moment came to me when I went to visit my stepfather-in-law, who I had been close to after he had been placed in a Hospice house, not by his choice. He told me he had no intention of dying. I had known him to be a kind man, somewhat gruff on the outside and a gentle soul who kept his personal pain inside. He functioned as an "in charge of everything in his life" guy. At the time of his going in the Hospice home, his wife was not speaking to me.

I heard from others that he was having a very difficult time there; not staying in bed, disoriented, removing all his clothing, pulling his foley catheter out and was VERY ANGRY at everyone. He had been drugged to keep him compliant. While I listened to what was happening with him, I made the decision to go to him the next day no matter what. My heart would not have it any other way.

I drove over the next morning; it was a beautiful spring morning with the birds singing and new life all around. The caregiver shared with me her joy that I was there to see him, as she stated that he was alone. When I walked into the room, the fear and anger were palpable. He was in bed, covered with a sheet and a blanket to his chin. Every muscle in his body was as tight as if he was fighting for his life in a battle with a very large individual. His fists were tightly clenched pushing up on his chin. His eyes were clenched shut, and his breathing was equally hard and distressed with flaring nares. His body almost jumped out of bed with each inhale and exhale; I counted his breath rate to be tachypnea at 24 per minute. He was not getting oxygen into his body.

I spoke softly letting him know that I was there as I moved a chair close to the bed and sat next to him, placing my hands first on his chest asking for his permission to be there and if I could offer assistance while telling him that he was loved and safe. I received a slight nudge of acknowledgment as I began to run energy. I continued running energy for over two hours. He gradually began to slow his breath in fifteen minutes and over time relaxed his hands, face and body. Over the next couple of hours, he completely relaxed and was breathing at a good rate. The room was full of love and peace.

I felt that it was the right time for me to go, not wanting to run into my mother-in-law, as I knew she would be disruptive for him.

I shared my love with him, hugged him and said my good-bye. I heard the next morning that he had passed over peacefully the night before.

It felt so very amazing to know that I was able to hold space for his release and help him move through his transition peacefully.

Energy healing has saved my life personally. Currently, with my RN license, I work with special needs individuals in their homes, writing up their assessments, protocols, and education and then training around the protocols I write. I am able to utilize my intuition and to hold the space for the families and my clients.

I have found what I can do in nursing with the families that I work closely with as a Holistic RN. My clients have become like family, after working with them for many years. I feel that it is impossible to work with an individual without looking at the complete picture, as it really does take a village. I also now know that it is time for me to move more fully into my energy work without the allopathic dictating.

Sharon Buller, BSN, RN

Sharon Buller received her Bachelor of Science in Nursing from Linfield College in 1994. Over the next four years, her career expanded from the hospital and clinics into the Public Health arena. In 1998, Sharon began her own business as an RN Consultant and expanded in 2002. She returned to Linfield as an Adjunct Clinical Instructor for three years. She continues her business, Aloha Holistic Wellness, today.

The truth of Energy Medicine, drew Sharon in, after being introduced to it while attending Linfield. Studying Dr. Bruce Lipton, *The Biology of Belief*, opened that truth completely in her world. Over the years, she has been drawn to and studied many modalities; beginning with Quantum Touch, Body Talk, Body Talk Access, Access Consciousness, Access Consciousness BARs, Crystals and Chakra Healing, Donna Eden's Energy Medicine, and Matrix Energetics. Sharon is a Psych-K Coach, a MBTI Certified Coach, and Energy Medicine Life Coach. She utilizes tools that support the body healing itself such as Sound Vitality, Crystal bowls, trinfinity8, Redox Signaling Molecules, Bemer, flower essences, and oils.

Sharon has three beautiful grown children and a kitty who adopted her two years ago, just as her seventeen-year-old loving cat passed on. Her love is sharing the outdoors with Mother Nature and her significant other; hiking, kayaking, camping, and reading.

"Love goes very far beyond the physical person of the beloved. It finds its deepest meaning in his spiritual being, his inner self. Whether or not he is actually present, whether or not he is still alive at all, ceases somehow to be of importance."

—Viktor E. Frankl, Man's Search for Meaning

A TRANSCENDENTAL LOVE

ANITA C. STEWART, RN

My nursing career did not unfold in the usual way. As students, we were advised to get basic training on the medical floor first, but in my case, I did the opposite. While attending nursing school, I worked as an aide in the ER of a small community hospital in Southern California. The adrenalin rush gave me a high that was as addictive as morphine. I was hooked. When I graduated in 1978, hospitals were screaming for 'critical care' nurses: even offering 6-month critical care courses for new grads; almost unheard of before. I jumped at the opportunity to obtain solid training that fueled my future in nursing. However, a year in ICU was all I could endure; my heart and soul loved ER, so back I went.

Working in a Level One Trauma Center was an experience and education of a lifetime. The next obvious progression was flight nursing. The more dangerous and challenging, the more I got that rush. That is what fueled me early on.

We had a saying in ER; "Treat 'em and street 'em." The focus was to diagnosis, treat and move 'em' out, like herding cattle. There was little time to get to know my patients in any deep or meaningful way.

Suddenly, after my own near-fatal horse accident, I had a profound Spiritual experience that took me on an inward journey of the unknown and unseen worlds. ("An Unexpected Awakening," Life Sparks, Edition One) Awakening to boundless Love, caring, compassion, and serenity, became the new paradigm; not only for nursing but my life in general. I had changed.

I switched specialties many times looking for greater fulfillment and less stress: I worked in PACU (post-anesthesia care unit), then interventional radiology, then case management, and finally outpatient surgery centers. With each change I garnered more time to spend with patients, diving deeper into my True Essence, experiencing greater compassion and caring while gaining enormous fulfillment.

I grew into my gifts of Energy Healing and Intuition; a gift conveyed to me during my "Awakening Experience." At that time, Energy Healing was looked upon as being 'unscientific' by the medical community, and I became known as the "Woo Woo" nurse. Being connected to another human through deep love and compassion ignited my nursing career. Compassion is the essence of nursing. I marveled at how patients responded, seeing better outcomes in every area. Finding many avenues of practicing Energy Medicine with not only patients but now private clients blessed me with a deep gratitude for life that stirred my soul.

Leaving the big city behind, I moved to a small town in Oregon. I easily found work at the hospital, but it took some time to adjust to the Medical Unit after being in critical care for so long. The challenges were many. It was a stressful classroom, but I grew and learned much.

Typically understaffed and overtasked for the amount of time allotted, it was a stretch to find time to do Energy work with my patients. But when I did, it opened up an avenue of healing that was not being addressed by allopathic medicine. By treating the whole person, patient outcomes improved. I saw blood pressures drop, anxiety relieved, fears released, and an overall greater acceptance of their situation; not to mention the reprieve from an overuse of call lights. My passion grew with each patient that experienced the energy work, and finding more ways to bring in the holistic approach became my mission. I was even running energy on my co-workers, bringing them some peace and balance. We all loved it. However, it was when I used this holistic approach with one patient something magical happened.

David and Julie Waterman were happily married, and deeply in love. They lived in a small town in Oregon where David was an attorney in Real Estate law. Well known and respected for protecting the natural resources, representing neighbors in land use disputes, he championed the community he loved. Sailing and playing piano were his forms of release while hiking, kayaking, and walks along the river where he lived brought him deep peace. Keeping in excellent shape, and looking like the epitome of health, one would have never guessed how his life was about to change.

The abdominal pain that sent him to Urgent Care that May, was initially thought to be Diverticulitis, an inflammation of the colon. Testing proved otherwise. The CT scan showed a mass in his right kidney, some nodules in both lungs, spots in the liver, and swollen lymph nodes: all indicating cancer. Biopsies later confirmed it. His symptoms were atypical, and confusing to his doctor.

"David, your biopsies were positive for cancer, but we really don't have a clue where it started. You probably have had this for some time as it is a body-wide problem," articulated the doctor. It was already stage IV at diagnosis. There are times in life when the unimaginable weight of the moment suspends reality in a surreal, heart-clamping silence. Stunned, the mind furiously searches for solutions that, one by one, fall by the wayside. Still in shock, David and Julie began a barrage of questions. Being intelligent folks, they took copious notes of everything relayed to them.

"Carcinoma of unknown origin," Julie wrote down on one of the many pages in her spiral notebooks. What came next was a plethora of testing to narrow down the primary starting point. Blood tests, tumor markers, x-rays and scans of every kind. Was this stomach or pancreas in origin? All they knew for sure was it was acting in an "aggressive manner." "Just trying to find the 'best recipe' for treatment," reported his physician. They changed ingredients like adding herbs to soup.

Diagnosis for them was not the end, but the beginning of a battle of epic proportion. The months from June to the following year in February were jammed with appointments, tests, chemotherapy infusions, 3-hour trips to Portland, more tests: ad nauseum. With every office visit, Julie's scribbled notes kept careful track of every minute detail, including his weight. He went from a healthy 168 pounds to 132 by the time I cared for him on the medical unit.

It was unusual to be assigned the same patient three consecutive days in a row. Normally we were bounced around causing continuity of care to suffer. Fortunately for me, I was assigned David's room three out of the seven days of his admission. The first time I entered his room I noticed a bright aliveness in his eyes, though his yellow skin and cachectic body told a different story. Opening myself to the quiet desperation of perfect strangers their immediate need for a miracle was apparent. Still fighting for his life, not ready to give up, he clung to anything that held any hope for wellness. Just by offering an aromatherapy diffuser in the room his spirit was lifted. It took such a small effort, but his smile brought such joy to my heart. Seeing this, I pursued conversations with he and his wife around the Spiritual and emotional aspects of David's prognosis. They were so open. They still had hope and said they believed in miracles. He was just not ready to leave his body at this young age of 59.

During one of our long talks, I shared my own near-death experience with them.

"It's a miracle I am alive today," I started out. "It was an experience that is difficult to put into words, and I would never be afraid to die again. The love I felt on the other side was palpable...like nothing I have ever experienced before. There are no words that can adequately describe it" I did my best to share something unknowable, and relief swept over their faces as I finished the story. Answering their questions about my experience and the beliefs I have about death now, brought a new-found peace to them. Grace filled the room that day as we grew closer. They thanked me for sharing.

Seeing how much this meant to them filled my heart with gratitude… grateful that I had the time to spend and make this horrible disease a little easier to endure. Normally, I would be running my tail off caring for 3-4 additional patients, but the call lights were quiet. It was apparent that the angels were watching over David and Julie.

It was a miracle that there was some free time to 'run energy' with David on several days. I explained how the biofield contains our personal energy and can become stagnant or blocked causing illness and dis-ease in our bodies. Healing Touch/Therapeutic Touch is a sacred healing art supporting our energy system, the life-sustaining force within each human being. The beauty of it is, nothing needs to be done except allow one's self to be a conduit. Anyone can learn it.

David gave his permission, and I began the session; centering my heart, aromatherapy diffusing, doors closed, lights dim, an ambiance of peace and love filled the room. My intuition peaked; my senses were on high; the energy was potent. I worked towards relieving his pain and balancing his chakras (energy centers). He was sitting in a chair and open to receive the energy, looking like someone receiving "Holy Communion." He offered no resistance, allowing the energy to flow powerfully, deepening his experience. I had no attachment to the results, got my personality and ego out of the way, while simultaneously acknowledging the mystery of Divine Intelligence that knows where the energy needs to go, the session continued for some time. At the completion, David returned to bed with a smile; relief appeared in his relaxed facial muscles. He slept peacefully, and his pain subsided.

Julie was forever by his side. She arrived early and left late. Appearing tired and worn out, I offered to do a little energy balancing on her, and she accepted. It repeatedly occurred to me how unusual it was for time to be made available for this. It gave us all a chance to connect in a deep and meaningful way and touched all our hearts. I was able to learn more about who David was, and how this terrible disease was tearing this family apart. I would go home and cry, praying some miracle would be forthcoming. The miracle came, though not as I expected.

David was discharged with home health, but not before the AIM (Advanced Illness Management) team was consulted, putting him on the palliative care program. I remember hearing David say, "If I have to depend on others to care for me, then I want all care to stop." He knew how much it was tearing his wife apart, especially the discussion about signing a "DNR" (Do Not Resuscitate). His love for Julie showed in everything he said and did.

It was only two weeks later when they readmitted him to the hospital. Arriving in the ER, weak and unable to walk, his labs showed acute renal failure and dehydration. My phone rang. It was Julie. "Could you come down to the hospital right away and do some more of that healing work on David," she asked. "Of course, Julie, I'll come right over," was my response.

On their last admission, we had grown close. There was something very special about this man. I arrived at the hospital feeling such honor to be able to do something for David that had given him relief prior. It was a sunny day in March. Their room was the same one he had been in previously...interesting! There was a difference this time; not having other patients to care for, my mind was very quiet. Focusing only on David's needs the energy vibrated through me with such intensity, it felt like I had grabbed an electric socket.

David received the energy openly, drinking it in like a thirsty desert dweller. The room was quiet, the energy palpable. When the session was complete, David looked straight into my eyes and said, "Thank you so much. I love you." I felt it to my core. My heart swelled; my eyes teared up; his words were penetrating. Then Julie spoke softly, "You are an angel." Something powerful was moving in this room.

Back in bed, David asked, "What should we be doing now, Anita?" The answer flowed naturally... "Sharing all the love you have for each other without holding anything back." With that said, Julie got up and walked over to his bed and sat next to him. I watched as they hugged, kissed and held each other tight, as if for the last time. Then it happened...

I know what I saw. I know what I was feeling... it was ethereal; a brilliantly bright, golden-white light blasted into the room, and with it came a 'peace that surpassed all understanding.' Awestruck, surreal, without words, I just sat there staring into this light of love, incontrovertible love. Julie later described the experience as "transcendental." It was the highest joy of my life to witness the beautiful light of their love for one another in that moment. It left me forever transformed. I left the room, the two of them embraced by this state of enlightenment. It resonates in my heart, still.

Though I could not attend David's memorial, this experience touched me, changed me in ways that are difficult to articulate. I came away with the most striking realization; the experiential knowing of the power of compassion and love transmitted through Healing Touch. It made such a difference to David and to Julie....and to me.

Death IS the great equalizer. Everything else of seeming importance fades away when life is hanging by a thread. In surrender, nothing stands in the way of Boundless Love, in all its expressions. It transcends even death.

Anita C. Stewart, RN, and Compiler of Nurse SPARKS

In hindsight, it's apparent that healing was something Anita was born into. As a child, working with sick or injured animals just came naturally to her. Birds with broken wings or dogs with injured legs, Anita would lay her hands on them and nurse them back to health. Riding horses from the time she could barely walk, she later became a competitive horsewoman. Anita had her sights set on becoming a veterinarian, but destiny took her to nursing, which was probably the best decision of her life.

Graduating from Los Angeles Pierce College, Woodland Hills, California in 1978 catapulted Anita into a fabulous 40-year nursing career that granted her sacred fulfillment. Her years working in emergency medicine, flight nursing, and critical care laid a solid foundation to be able to work, pretty much, anywhere she choose.

After sustaining critical injuries from a horse accident in 1981 ("An Unexpected Awakening," *LifeSPARKS, Edition One,* it was revealed to Anita that the time had come to share her healing gifts with others. Using hands-on energy healing was looked upon as pseudo-science in the 80's, and just becoming known through leaders like Rev. Rosalyn L. Bruyere, Barbara Brennan, (Barbara Brennan's School of Healing), and Dolores Krieger (Therapeutic Touch). Although she read some of their books, it was Grace that moved through Anita as she surrendered to the ONE. Allowing ego and personality to step aside, the Energy knows exactly where to go and does the work. Anita's only intention is to be the clearest channel for Grace to show up in.

Her private practice in Bend, Oregon, "Bridges of the Heart," endowed her with some of the most transcendental experiences, stirring the soul. Seeing her clients release the stuck patterns that block their awakening to Essence is truly awe-inspiring. The combination of 40 years in nursing and energy medicine instilled tremendous insights and intuition that enhance the wellness of those drawn to Anita's work. Her passion is to help bridge energy medicine with mainstream medicine. It is only through dedicated and persistent research, study and refinement of these modalities that the world will welcome it with open arms.

Anita dedicates her life to the beautiful energies that hasten healing from the physical and beyond. It is with deep devotion to healing, not only the physical but mental and spiritual levels as well that she rests in the perfection of the energy to know the way. People often ask what she calls the energy work that comes through her. The only answer that seems true is this, "You can't put God in a box." As soon as it is named, it takes it out of the mystery and into the madness and control of the egoic mind.

Anita is available for healing sessions either in person or by phone. She welcomes you to give it a try.

www.bridgesoftheheart.com

anitastewart@bridgesoftheheart.com

Acknowledgements

We would like to express our profound gratitude to the sixteen authors of this book for their contribution. It has been an absolute joy and pleasure to walk this journey with them. Each one holds a special place in our heart; they inspired us to fulfill our purpose, as we collaborated with them to expand theirs. They came here as separate authors, but left as a part of the *Nurse SPARKS* family.

This book would not be in your hands, if not for the heart and soul of Anita Stewart. The love and power contained in the pages of this book starts with her. It was her vision that brought this project to fruition. We were just the vessel for her spirit to take shape in the form of this book. We appreciate her beyond words and are grateful to her for her work as the compiler of these amazing stories.

We thank Catherine VanWetter for interviewing our authors, and offering them an opportunity to share more of who they are on Authentic Messengers Radio. She made them comfortable and confident in expressing themselves through their audio recordings.

We all acknowledge our families for their unconditional love and support. Their patience through this process has been invaluable!

And finally, we thank all the visionaries and change-makers that have entrusted us to support them over the past several years. You are the inspiration that seeded this vision. There would be no SPARKS series without you!

Tami, Allison, Denise and Dan
Your SPARKS Team
Positive Media Ventures, LLC

A New Era of Story Sharing is Born!

We are taking applications for future *Nurse SPARKS* books.

Our SPARKS book series is publishing stories that illuminate, inspire, and ignite hearts.

Your Story Matters. You Matter!

Learn how you can participate in our SPARKS program and have your story published in a SPARKS book.

Our professionals manage the details. You receive the beauty of learning from us, as you live your publishing dream.

- Connect with our SPARKS team to chat about what you would attempt to write... if you could! With the help of a professional team, find out how you can!
- Gain knowledge and skills through an experiential, proven program and author bonus benefits.

For information on contributing to a future Nurse SPARKS book, email Anita Stewart, RN: anitastewart@bridgesoftheheart.com

For information on sponsoring your own SPARKS series, or compiling an anthology, email Tami Blodgett: tami@AuthenticMessengers.com

Visit these websites for more information and to read more about our authors:

www.AuthenticMessengers.com

www.positivemediapress.com

https://www.facebook.com/ SPARKSofInspiration/

https://twitter.com/Sparks2Inspire

http://www.authenticmessengers.com/radio-podcast

Meet the SPARKS Team
Your Success is Our Success

TAMI BLODGETT

Co-Creator SPARKS Program
Managing Director, Positive Media Press
Chief Visionary Officer, Positive Media Ventures
www.positivemediapress.com

Tami is the one with all the big ideas! She is a respected mentor, coach and strategist who tirelessly serves those who yearn to make a real difference in the world. Tami has supported hundreds of change-makers in bringing their message to a global audience through writing, radio, speaking and program creation. She gently guides the people she supports to be seen and heard in a way that is in alignment with their values and personal truth. It is her true calling to create and build platforms that empower messengers to uncover their vision and make that vision a reality. "Just BE." This is Tami's mantra that keeps her in alignment with her true self.

"Our chief want is someone who will inspire us to be what we know we could be."
—Ralph Waldo Emerson

ALLISON SAIA

Co-Creator SPARKS Program
Publishing Director, Positive Media Press
Chief Creative Officer, Positive Media Ventures
www.positivemediapress.com

Allison is the creative heart of Positive Media Press. She prides herself as a professional wordsmith and a highly effective writing coach. She is the one that makes everything look and sound good. With over 27 years of writing and editing experience, Allison brings a wealth of knowledge and expertise to our company. Her passion is helping her clients find their voice, and guiding them, hand in hand, in their writing journey. Allison hopes that by helping people find their story, she helps them find themselves in the process. She is a best-selling author and poet and is a former Poet Laureate of Hanover, Pennsylvania.

"Books are the mirrors of the soul."
—Virginia Woolf

DENISE BEINS

Co-Creator SPARKS Program
Chief Organizational Officer, Positive Media Ventures
www.positivemediapress.com

Denise keeps us all sane! She's been keeping schedules and organizing since she was a little girl growing up on a farm. Denise is a master project manager who believes that good systems help companies run smoothly and allow teams to work more effectively. Denise takes care of all the countless details that keep our business visible and thriving, and able to help more messengers in getting their stories out to the world. The company culture the she maintains empowers our team to utilize their strengths and passions.

"Efforts and courage are not enough without purpose and direction."
—John F. Kennedy

DAN SAIA

Co-Creator SPARKS Program
Media Director, Inspirational Talk Radio
Chief Innovation Officer, Positive Media Ventures
www.positivemediapress.com

Dan is our "Jack of All Trades." A seasoned IT and sales professional, he is the one who keeps our websites running and handles all the backend techy stuff. A master communicator, Dan is committed to serving our clients in a way that is knowledgeable, but personable. He is always on top of new trends and keeps us on the cutting edge. When we need something done around here, Dan is the guy we know can handle anything--from fixing a website to fixing a car, and anything in between.

*"Have the courage to follow your heart and intuition.
They somehow know what you truly want to become."*
—Steve Jobs

ANITA C. STEWART

Compiler, Nurse SPARKS
Founder, Bridges of the Heart Programs
http://bridgesoftheheart.com/

Anita C. Stewart, R.N., has been gifted to work in healing her whole life. First experienced as a child tending to sick and injured animals, she went on to earn her nursing degree in 1978, with high level hospital nursing as her career for 40 years. Her own debilitating injury initiated a series of events that naturally led her to expand her abilities to help others, physically, emotionally and spiritually—not through her own knowledge and power, but through surrender to a power greater than her own. Her passion is to bridge Energy Medicine with Mainstream medicine through her private practice "Bridges of the Heart" where she treats clients, teaches classes and speaks to groups.

"When our eyes see our hands doing the work of our hearts, the circle of creation is completed inside of us, the doors of our souls fly open and love steps forth to heal everything in sight."
—Michael Bridge

Made in the USA
Columbia, SC
25 May 2017